False Albacore

False Albacore

A Comprehensive Guide
to Fly Fishing's Hottest Fish

Tackle, Baitfish, Flies,
Seasonal Hot Spots,
and Techniques

Tom Gilmore

The Countryman Press
Woodstock, Vermont

Library of Congress Cataloging-in-Publication Data
Gilmore, Tom, 1946-
    False albacore : a comprehensive guide to fly fishing's hottest fish / Tom Gilmore.— 1st ed.
    p. cm.
    ISBN 0-88150-520-X
    1. Tuna fishing—Atlantic Coast (U.S.) 2. Euthynnus alletteratus. I. Title.

SH691.T8 G56 2002
799.1'7782—dc21

2002067269

Interior design by Faith Hague
Cover design by Johnson Design
Cover photograph by Jim Levison
Illustrations by Barbara Smullen
Maps by Paul Woodward, © 2002 The Countryman Press
Photo on page 17 by Tom Gilmore
Photo on page 125 by Ed Jaworowski

Published by The Countryman Press, P.O. Box 748, Woodstock, Vermont 05091

Distributed by W.W. Norton & Company, 500 Fifth Avenue, New York, NY 10110

Printed in the United States of America

10 9 8 7 6 5 4 3 2 1

To Dad

*While not a fisherman, he always made time
to take me fishing and was good enough
to make me think he enjoyed it.*

Contents

Acknowledgments

Over the years, so many people have contributed to my knowledge and enjoyment of the sport of saltwater fly fishing and to the production of this manuscript. I wish I could individually thank each and every one of them, but time and space does not allow. So let me first thank the anglers, tiers, and friends not mentioned below.

I wish to extend my deepest gratitude to Ed Janiga, who believed in me even before I did and gave me the courage to start this project in the first place. He was there every step of the way, providing encouragement and support. Ed, I couldn't have done it without you.

I also want to thank Captain Steve Bellefleur for guiding me to my first false albacore and bonito and for sharing his incredible knowledge gained from a lifetime of on-the-water observations. Steve, you're simply the best. See you on the water.

A special thanks to lifelong friend and mentor, Ed Jaworowski, not only for taking the stunning color images of the flies that appear in the book, but for sharing his knowledge and insight and friendship.

I am grateful to Tim Harper for his early guidance and advice on how to approach this project and for providing valuable lessons along the way. Brian Schneider for his help with the illustrations, and Phil DiVuolo for his thoughtful suggestions on early drafts.

Captain Joe Keegan, for the countless hours we shared together chasing these magnificent creatures. Fishing partners Bill Ryan, Steve Murphy, Joe DiBello, Lenny Maiorano, Matt Toomey, Mitch Nottingham, and Lee Schisler, who have chased false albacore with me from the Cape to the Keys. Thanks, guys, for the good times and the memories.

Dave Skok, who shared his enthusiasm and tips for landing false albacore from shore; tips that helped Dave win the prestigious Martha's Vineyard Derby. Dave also provided many of the images in this book and introduced me to his soon-to-be-classic fly pattern, the Mushmouth. Bob Lindquist, for sharing his wealth of knowledge of baitfish, their habits, and how to imitate them in fishing and fly tying. Teddy Patlen, for help in obtaining several of the original flies featured in this book, and for just being "Teddy."

The crew at Ramsey Outdoors, Stuart Levine, Bill Tomiello, and John Roetman, for their ongoing commitment to promoting the sport of fly fishing through their annual series of educational seminars. These seminars are free to all and are dedicated to increasing our knowledge and enjoyment of the sport. I have had the pleasure of participating as a presenter and a student.

To Tom Earnhardt, who introduced so many of us to the world-class false albacore fishery off Harkers Island, North Carolina. Tom, thanks for sharing your backyard with other albie chasers and for your thoughtful help and suggestions.

Captain Scott Hamilton, for opening my eyes to the tremendous run of "bonito" along the southeast coast of Florida.

To Lefty Kreh, Bob Clouser, and Bob Popovics, not only for the killer fly patterns you have given us, but also for your willingness to share your knowledge. There aren't three better ambassadors for any sport; real pros that enjoy nothing more than helping a novice improve his game.

I have had the pleasure of fishing with some of the finest guides on the East Coast. This book was made possible in large part because of their willingness to share their experiences and "hot spots" with me. I also want to acknowledge the many shop owners, fly tiers, biologists, and fishermen that were good enough to grant me an interview.

For help with Martha's Vineyard, I want to offer my gratitude to Jamie Boyle, Leslie Smith, Ken and Lori Vanderlaske, Tim Flarity, and Greg Shomol; Mike Monte, Hal Herrick, Lynne Heyer, and Bill Pew for their help with the Nantucket fishery; and Greg Wiesel and Bob Paccia for sharing their knowledge of the South Cape.

For information along the Rhode Island and Connecticut shoreline, I wish to thank Peter Jenkins, Jim White, Don Rafferty, Pete Farrell, Steve Bellefleur, Steve Burnett, Dan Wood, Joe Keegan, and Eric Peterson.

For help with the New York/New Jersey fishery, Paul Dixon, Barry Kanavy, David Blinken, Jim Levison, John McMurray, David Azar, John Killen, Scott Holder, Bob Robl, Dino Torino, Dave Chouinard, Bill Hoblitzell, Gene Quigley, Paul Eidman, John Costello, and John Roteman.

The chapter on North Carolina's Outer Banks would not have been possible without Tom Earnhardt, Brian Horsley, Sara Gardner, Joe Shute, Dave Dietzler, Adrian Goodwin, Jr., Gordon Churchill, Tom Wagner, and Dave Rhode.

For help on the southeast coast of Florida, in addition to Scott Hamilton, I'd like to thank Scott Hofmeister, Cliff Budd, Greg Bogdan, David Fawcett, Mark Houghtaling, and Edan White.

I am grateful to Kermit Hummel and the rest of the staff at Countryman Press for giving an unknown author and a little-known fish the opportunity to tell their stories. For his crisp editing of my early drafts, I'd like to thank my colleague, Walter Keonig.

But most of all I want to thank my wife, Joanne. As my lifelong partner, Joanne has always generously supported my passion for fishing. She partnered in this project every step of the way, from booking guides as surprise birthday presents to reading and editing drafts, then questioning, editing, and reading again. I also want to thank my three lovely daughters, Jennifer, Julie, and Christina, as well as my sons-in-law, Darren and Bryan, for their enthusiasm and encouragement in this project, but most of all for giving me two beautiful grandchildren, Jack and Ashley.

The author with a false albacore off Stonington, Connecticut

Introduction

The Boys of Autumn

Inching his way through the damp fog that warm autumn morning, Captain Steve Bellefleur cut the engine on his 19-foot Mako to listen for the bell buoy that would mark the reef and associated rips that we were targeting for the morning bite. As the engine noise began to subside, Steve said, "Do you hear that?" Having birded the Northeast coast for the last 20 years, I easily recognized the screams of herring gulls. "Herring gulls, lots of them," I responded. "Happy herring gulls," Steve replied. "And do you know why they're happy? 'Cause they're over false albacore and not those toothy bluefish."

As we drifted closer to the gulls, I began to hear the violent eruptions of "albies" greyhounding through the masses of bay anchovies that were being sucked down-tide. I could see white spray being thrown in every direction as albies crashed through the terrified baitfish, sending them flying in every direction and then falling back into the frenzy like wind-driven raindrops.

I grabbed my 10-weight fly rod, hands trembling, stomach churning, and somehow managed a 60-foot cast into the melee. Two short strips of fly line and something with the speed and strength of a thoroughbred had taken my offering. The fly line exploded off the deck, flying through the guides at breakneck speed. I tried to slow the line with my thumb and index finger, but an instant inch-long gash halted that strategy. Within a few accelerated heartbeats, the fly line melted from my reel and turned into backing. Seconds later, I noticed the 100-yard marking on my backing as it sailed through the guides of my fly rod.

Then, the dreaded signal that brings on the worst feeling in all of fishing—slack line. After a blistering 100-yard sprint, the line went dead. But my frustration, along with that sinking feeling of failure, was interrupted by Steve's shout, "Reel, dammit, reel!" A few frantic seconds of winding, and the line tightened. The fish was back, and it was mad as hell. Now it was ripping off line up-current into the fog.

Eventually, the runs grew shorter as the fish began to tire. I was able to turn it back toward the boat and slowly begin to take control of the fight. As the fly line came back through the guides and onto the reel, I could put more pressure on the fish. When it neared the boat it began to circle in the dark depths below. Following Steve's advice, I would lift up as hard as I dared and then wind down, repeating the motion—lift up, wind down. Inch by grudging inch, I unscrewed the circling fish from the depths of the ocean. At times, my rod strained so hard it resembled a fully-drawn archer's bow.

After what seemed like an eternity, Steve grabbed the fish at the front of its powerful tail and hoisted it over the gunwale. Exhausted but ecstatic, I sank back into the bow seat and let out a holler of relief and exhilaration. I sat there shaking my head in disbelief at the speed and power this fish had just displayed. Steve quickly released it and asked a question to which he already knew the answer: "So, how do you like fishing for the Boys of Autumn?" After I caught my breath and stopped shaking, I realized that I had just encountered a fish that I would never get enough of. Hook one of these ocean speedsters and you will catch albie fever. The only cure? Another albie!

Ever since that autumn morning in the rips off Watch Hill, Rhode Island, I have been consumed with pursuing this fish. I had so many questions and at that time there were so few answers. Where do they come from? What causes them to arrive and disappear? Does water temperature or availability of food trigger their migration? How predictable are their appearances and feeding patterns? What makes them so much faster and stronger than other inshore game fish? Where else could they be found?

I began to read every article I could find, both in angling literature and in marine research libraries, in search of answers. I have chased them on Massachusetts' Cape Islands, Rhode Island's breachways, the rips off Connecticut, the forks of Long Island, and the Jersey beaches. I have made pilgrimages to Cape Lookout in North Carolina and extended the fishing season by chasing them on both coasts of the Florida Peninsula. In each of these locations, I have had the pleasure of fishing with and interviewing some of the finest guides and dedicated fly fishermen on the East Coast. In the pages that follow, I try to share what I have learned in the hope that you, the reader, will join the growing group of anglers that treasures the sport of angling for this spectacular fish. When we reach a critical mass of constituents, perhaps we will have the political clout to elevate false albacore to a "game fish" status with the protection they deserve.

I still love the rise of a selective brown trout, the tenacity of bluefish, and the gill-rattling aerial displays of tarpon. I still enjoy my winter retreat to the warm bonefish flats of a Caribbean island to stalk the skinny water in search of the ghosts of the flats. The new moon in June will still find me fishing a beach along the Northeast coast, as striped bass suck in diminutive sand eels in the pre-dawn hours. But all of that for me is just spring training in preparation for doing battle with "The Boys of Autumn."

Part I

Fly Fishing's Hottest Fish

Saltwater
Fly Fishing

1

The Early Days

I recall standing on the beach at North Bar in the shadow of the light-house that marks Montauk Point on Long Island's south fork. The first light of false dawn had begun to reveal silhouettes of striper fishermen who had taken their position in the picket line that had formed in the dark of that October new moon. They were there to fish the rip that was caused by the dropping tide rushing over the sandbar. As the sun began to rise, the shapes became clearer, and I suddenly realized I was the only fly fisherman on the beach. The year was 1985, and the veteran Montauk pluggers were not subtle in their disdain for my style of fishing.

Later that morning, back in town, I stopped at one of the local tackle shops where the manager and several regulars were outside admiring a 50-pound cow bass that had been taken on bait from under the Montauk Lighthouse. After the fish was weighed and the successful angler con-gratulated, I wandered back inside the shop, trying my best to fit in with the group. I purchased a few items I didn't need, standard practice before asking for free advice, and casually inquired, "Where would you suggest is a good place to fly fish?" "Where you from?" the manager asked. "New Jersey," I responded. "Well, why don't you go back home and give it a try!" Amid the raucous laughter, I grabbed my change, smiled politely, and slid out the side door. Less than three years later that same manager was selling fly rods and advertising himself as a fly-fishing guide.

There have been pockets of saltwater fly fishermen along the Atlantic coast, most notably the Saltwater Fly Rodders of America, founded in

Bob Clouser with a false albacore that fell for his Clouser Minnow

1962 in Elwood "Cap" Colvin's tackle shop in Seaside Park, New Jersey. But in the early 1980s, with the exception of the Florida Keys, saltwater fly fishermen were still a rare breed. There was very little written information on our sport. Equipment was cumbersome and fly patterns were very basic. Stripping baskets got very strange looks from other anglers on the beach.

The Explosion

In the last fifteen years, the popularity of East Coast saltwater fly fishing has exploded, and it is now the fastest growing segment of the fly fishing industry. There are several reasons for the increased interest in the sport, but the comeback of the striped bass ranks at the top. Successful fisheries management practices and harvest limits have brought this magnificent creature back from the brink. We now have a viable game fish available to coastal fly fishermen for most of the year. Spice this up with sporadic bluefish blitzes in our inshore waters for up to six months of the year, and it's easy to see why fishing with the long rod is becoming a common sight on the beaches of the East Coast.

With increased angling opportunities, the economics of supply and demand began to deliver new technologies to coastal anglers. Modern materials have made rods light enough for fishermen to withstand the strain of hours of blind casting big flies into the wind. Improved drag systems on reels can withstand the long powerful runs of ocean game fish. Specialty lines were developed with aggressive front tapers designed to turn over big flies into the wind with a minimum of false casts. Building on the pioneering work of legends like Joe Brooks, Frank and Harold Gibbs, Frank Woolner, Bob Clouser, Lou Tabory, and Lefty Kreh, innovative fly tiers like Bob Popovics, Eric Peterson, Bob Lindquist, and David Skok are using modern synthetic materials, epoxy, and silicone to produce a whole new generation of "match-the-hatch" concept flies that look real, are easy to cast, and can withstand the rigors of the salt.

Today, we have a well-equipped army of flyrodders plying the coast in search of striped bass and bluefish. These fishermen are accustomed to catch-and-release fishing. Some gravitated to saltwater fly fishing from freshwater, where many of our better streams have gone catch-and-release in order to provide quality recreational angling. Others remember plugging the surf, where the size limits on striped bass had them practicing catch-and-release.

Fly-rod catches of bass and blues have become common, and flyrodders are often racking up impressive numbers of these species. As fishermen become more successful, they look for new challenges to test their skills and to increase their enjoyment of the sport. First, it's bigger numbers of fish. The next challenge is bigger fish, then selective fish, and finally, a great fighting fish.

The Blitz

Today, the talk of every coastal fly fisherman from Massachusetts' Cape Islands to North Carolina's Outer Banks is the fall false albacore blitz. This occurs somewhere along the Atlantic coast from August until December when water temperatures drop into the 60s, sending baitfish funneling out of our tidal estuaries on their southern migration. Inlets or offshore rips that carry massive schools of bait are likely locations for blitzing albacore. Blitzing fish are not hard to locate; usually, the first sign is distant clouds of densely-packed birds. Wheeling gulls and diving terns are good indicators. As you get closer to the blitz, you'll hear the gulls screaming and see the surface explosions of albacore busting through schools of bait, sending white water and showering baitfish high into the air. The sight of any surface-feeding game fish is welcome, but the sound of surface-feeding false albacore is thrilling. You can actually hear the sharp sizzling sound they make as they slice through the water devouring anything in their path.

Blitzing fish will readily take a well-presented subsurface fly, but my choice for blitzing albies is a surface popper. There is no better sight or sound than that of a 12-pound tuna blasting from out of nowhere at 40 mph to crush a popper in a shower of white water. Simply put, these fish are the fastest, toughest, and most challenging inshore fish on the East Coast. I suggest you give them a try, and I guarantee you'll never forget your first!

False Albacore, the Fish

False albacore (*Euthynnus alletteratus*) and true tunas belong to the same family as mackerel, Scombridae. Fisheries management personnel officially recognize *Euthynnus alletteratus* by the common name "little tunny" to distinguish this red-fleshed mackerel from the white-fleshed tuna we call Albacore (*Thunnus alalunga*). Little tunny at one time were included in the genus *Thunnus*, but it was felt that there were enough differences between them and the other "tunas" to place them in a separate genus, *Euthynnus*.

The name little tunny has yet to catch on with the fly-fishing fraternity, who refer to them as false albacore, albies, or Fat Alberts. In Florida, they are misleadingly referred to as "bonito." They are frequently confused with their inshore cousin, the Atlantic bonito (*Sarda sarda*). While similarly shaped, the latter are only a little more than half the size of false albacore and their markings are different. Bonito have fairly straight horizontal stripes on their backs, with dark vertical patches on their sides. False albacore have blue-green backs with horizontal, irregular, mackerel-type markings and chrome sides and white bellies. Their most distinguishing markings are the three to five dark spots that look like fingerprints below their pectoral fins on an otherwise all-white belly.

Built for Speed

Like all members of the tuna family, false albacore are a highly migratory, pelagic fish built for speed. They are hydrodynamic marvels, with torpedo-shaped bodies, retractable dorsal fins, and side depressions for their

TOM GILMORE

False albacore are built for speed

pectoral fins that enable them to greatly reduce their hydrodynamic drag. Other body features include smooth "frictionless" skin that is covered with mucous to reduce drag and a powerful rudder-like tail that can cycle at a speed of up to 30 times per second, a blur to the human eye. Members of the tuna family are nearly all muscle, with upwards of 75 percent of their body weight being muscle mass compared to less than 40 percent for most fish.

Most fish are cold-blooded, which means their internal body temperature matches that of the surrounding water. Tuna, swordfish, and marlin are warm-blooded and can maintain an internal temperature higher than the surrounding water. The advantage of a higher internal temperature is that it allows for a higher metabolism. Warmer muscles can also contract faster than cold muscles, permitting warm-blooded fish to swim faster after their prey. Tuna have large blood volumes, with the highest proportion of oxygen known among fish, and a concentration of hemoglobin as high as that of humans. The gill surface area of the tuna is the highest among all fish, and they have a respiratory capacity that approaches that of humans. Since fast swimmers require substantial energy, it follows that the metabolic rates of tuna are also the highest known among all fish. False albacore swim with open mouths, letting water rush through their gills and then along the sides of the body, reducing turbulence and increasing the streamline effect. Grooves along the tongue direct the flow of water. Water rushing through the gills serves the high oxygen needs of false albacore.

It's no wonder that false albacore are the fastest inshore fish and faster than many onshore creatures. At speeds of 40 miles per hour, false albacore are twice as fast as bluefish and 30 percent faster than bonefish.

Comparison of Speed (mph)

	10	20	30	40	50
Track Runner	—				
Horse	———				
Bluefish	———				
Bonefish	————————			
False Albacore	———————————			

Feeding Behavior

In addition to speed, the feeding behavior of false albacore offers another great challenge in presenting the fly. They will push bait to the surface, crash through a tightly-packed school of baitfish in just a few seconds, and then dive deep, only to pop up minutes later some distance away. Most fish have swim bladders that regulate buoyancy. The majority of the tuna species don't have swim bladders, so they can explode to the surface, crash bait, and dive deep in seconds. This up-and-down feeding behavior can be extremely frustrating for both shore and boat fishermen. They do, however, develop patterns and often repeat their feeding cycle. Bait, structure, and current are the keys to predicting where they will show up next.

Eye of an Eagle

As if speed and a sporadic feeding style don't offer enough of a challenge, tunas have keen eyesight and can be extremely selective. Fortunately, false albacore have little in the way of teeth, so a wire or shock tippet is unnecessary. Species with teeth, like bluefish and barracuda, often take chunks of prey that would be too big to swallow whole. Species without teeth, like striped bass and false albacore, must be able to take a bait whole. Unlike stripers, though, false albacore have relatively small mouths, so they normally target small baitfish. When albacore are being selective—and they usually are—I find size to be the most important factor in fly selection, followed by shape and then color.

Scientific studies have shown that inshore fish have good color vision, while offshore species such as albacore and dorado have monochromatic vision and respond best to blue and sometimes green. Fish with monochromatic vision can still see baits and flies of other colors, as they contrast with the surrounding water.

While I have caught false albacore on flies of many different colors, shapes and sizes, I prefer to match the predominant baitfish in an area as closely as I can. On calm, clear days, if the fish are refusing my offering, switching to patterns with some blue or green mixed in has saved the day on numerous occasions.

Nomads

False albacore are found on the East Coast from southern New England to the Florida Keys and the Gulf of Mexico. Scientists are now using new satellite tagging technology to unlock the mysteries of tuna migration. However, their research is being conducted on commercially important species such as the giant bluefin tuna, which can fetch as much as $50,000 per fish on the Tokyo seafood market. Over-harvesting has caused the breeding stocks of bluefin tuna in the western Atlantic to decline over 80 percent in the last 20 years.

Because of their poor food value, false albacore are not targeted by the commercial fishing industry, which should bode well for future conservation initiatives. For the same reason, very little research has been done on their growth rates, reproductive biology, and life history.

False albacore swim in the upper waters of the Gulf Stream, making seasonal pilgrimages inshore to feed on large concentrations of prey species. The Gulf Stream is an immense ocean-river of warm water that flows from the Gulf of Mexico through the Florida Straits and along the east coast of Florida, its closest point to shore. It then flows northeast, coming close to shore again along the Outer Banks of North Carolina. The Gulf Stream's waters are deep blue, with great clarity and high temperatures. It ranges from 50 to 90 miles wide at the surface. While I am not aware of any studies of false albacore migratory patterns, I suspect that they migrate both north and south along the coast, as well as east and west to and from the Gulf Stream. In the Northeast, they appear in late August or early September, peaking sometime between mid-September and mid-October, depending on water temperature and the avail-

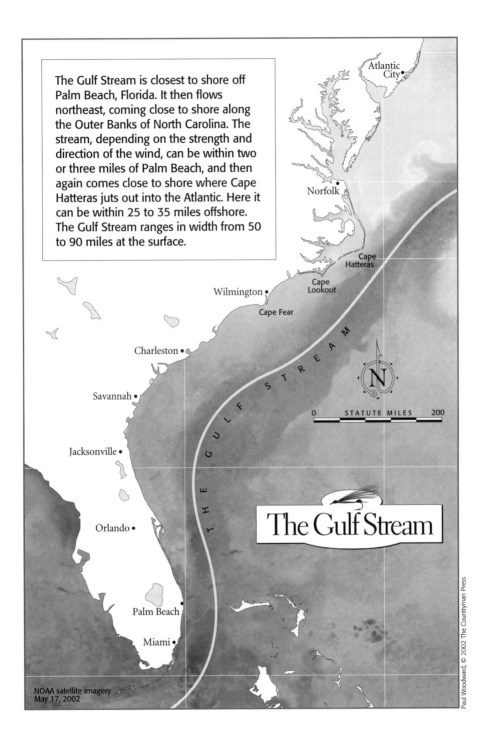

The Gulf Stream is closest to shore off Palm Beach, Florida. It then flows northeast, coming close to shore along the Outer Banks of North Carolina. The stream, depending on the strength and direction of the wind, can be within two or three miles of Palm Beach, and then again comes close to shore where Cape Hatteras juts out into the Atlantic. Here it can be within 25 to 35 miles offshore. The Gulf Stream ranges in width from 50 to 90 miles at the surface.

Atlantic City

Norfolk

Cape Hatteras

Cape Lookout

Wilmington

Cape Fear

Charleston

Savannah

N

0   STATUTE MILES   200

Jacksonville

Orlando

The Gulf Stream

Palm Beach

Miami

THE GULF STREAM

NOAA satellite imagery
May 17, 2002

Paul Woodward, © 2002 The Countryman Press

ability of prey species. In North Carolina, they usually arrive inshore in early October and stay into mid-December, with peak fishing often centered around the first two weeks in November.

For years, anglers assumed that the New England fish moved south to the Outer Banks as the water cooled in the north. But no one could explain the tremendous difference in fish size. The New England fish usually run under 10 pounds, with an occasional 12- to 14-pound fish in the mix. In North Carolina, the fish average 10 to 12 pounds, and catching a fish over 15 pounds is a daily possibility.

A few years ago, I started chasing false albacore off the east coast of Florida in the Palm Beach area, where the Gulf Stream is tightest to shore. Here, the fish arrive in the spring and peak in June and July before thinning out and heading northward with the Gulf Stream in August and September. Their size matches that of the North Carolina fish. My conclusion is that when the New England fish leave for warmer water, most of them move south and offshore to the Gulf Stream, while most of the fall run in North Carolina is comprised of resident offshore fish and fish from Florida. The largest fly-rod fish come annually from the east coast of Florida and the Outer Banks of North Carolina, the two areas closest to the Gulf Stream. By all accounts, both North Carolina and Florida have year-round, offshore resident fish.

Inshore Fishing Opportunities for False Albacore

	J	F	M	A	M	J	J	A	S	O	N	D
Southern New England								xxxXXXXxxx				
North Carolina			xxxxxxxxxx						xxXXXXXXxxxx			
East Coast of Florida				xxxxxxXXXXXXXXXXxxx								
Gulf Coast of Florida	xxxxxxxxxx		xxxxx									

x = Available
X = Peak

IGFA Tippet Class World Records

Tippet	Weight (lbs./oz.)	Location	Angler	Date
Male				
2	7/9	Bayhead, NJ	Ron Mazzarella	10/20/01
4	13/8	Key West, FL	Robert Bass	7/23/83
6	18/4	Cape Canaveral, FL	Dave Chermanski	7/24/72

8	17/8	Jupiter, FL	Andy Mill	7/7/96
12	17/12	Key West, FL	Luis de Hoyos	5/18/83
16	19/5	Cape Lookout, NC	Jim Rivers	11/9/00
20	19/0	Dry Tortugas, FL	Philip Caputo	4/12/95

Female

2	Vacant			
4	2/0	Miami, FL	Pamela Marmin	1/1/98
6	14/4	Key West, FL	Pamela Marmin	4/22/01
8	14/0	Key West, FL	Lisa Booth	5/2/00
12	15/4	Key West, FL	Jennifer Andreae	5/13/99
16	14/13	Key West, FL	Linda Gracie	4//29/00
20	15/8	Port Canaveral, FL	Christine Perez	8/17/00

Finding Fish

3

Shrink the Playing Field

The Atlantic Ocean can be an intimidating playing field, especially when one is armed only with a fly rod. I'll never forget the first time I attempted to fly fish in salt water. As I crested the last sand dune and could see the vast sea of blue in front of me, I looked down at my 8-weight outfit and then back at the daunting ocean and started to laugh. At that moment, the thought of tackling the ocean with a fly rod seemed ludicrous. I never did fish that day.

Now, I approach the sea with confidence because I have learned to "shrink the playing field." I do this by fishing inlets, breachways, rock jetties, points, bowls, and offshore reefs and rips. Any structure that will funnel current will deliver large concentrations of bait in a smaller, fishable area. Having come from a trout-fishing background, finding fish in salt water was my most difficult challenge.

I cut my fly-fishing teeth on north-central Pennsylvania's native brook trout streams. Good pools on those mountain streams hold fish year-round because the food supply is there. In salt water, game fish must constantly search for food by following the migratory patterns of prey. For anglers, finding baitfish is often more important than having the right fly. With a little homework, you can find the best locations to fish in your own region. Tackle shops, web sites, fishing clubs, and news articles can be very helpful in locating hot spots. The next step is to determine each hot spot's "happy hour," when the tide delivers the most bait to waiting predators. Again, most good tackle shops can help you with this, but here are some basics.

Got Bait?

When you find heavy concentrations of schooling bait, predators can't be far off. Study how the bait is reacting. If it appears nervous, showing lots of flashing sides or constantly changing direction, predators are often nearby. Nervous-looking water can result from bait being driven high in the water column by predators below. The tighter the bait is "balled up," or the closer it is to structure or the beach, the greater the likelihood that predators are present. Circling, jumping, or skipping bait or bait pushed up on the beach are dead giveaways that predators are on the feed.

Birds as Scouts

Birds are another good indicator of the presence of predators. The thing that I remember most about my first saltwater blitz was the staggering number of birds. While climbing the path over the dune, I could hear the raucous cries of gulls. As I reached the crest, I could see a tightly-bunched flock wheeling over the surf in front of me, dipping to pick wounded mullet from the shallows. Blues were slashing through the waves, cutting anything that moved in half. Screaming herring gulls were snatching baitfish that had beached themselves to avoid the jaws of bluefish. The slashing attacks by the bluefish and the feeding frenzy of the gulls combined to etch my first blitz into memory. Schools of false albacore also drive bait from the depths to the surface, making them available to birds. Flocks of birds are quite visible and vocal even at great distances. If you see birds leaving your area and heading off in one direction, it often pays to follow them. A large concentration of birds resting on the water or on the beach indicates their anticipation of a feeding spree.

As with baitfish, observe bird behavior carefully. A sudden turn, change of direction, or dip toward the surface can indicate the presence of fish. Watch their flying rhythm—a long, slow, relaxed wingbeat means they are looking for food; an excited, short, erratic pattern means they are on bait. Even a single circling bird can indicate albies below. Capt. Steve Bellefleur was the first to clue me in to the fact that birds often shadow albies, waiting for them to drive bait to the surface for an easy meal. During times of no visible surface activity, he often accurately predicted an albie hook-up by the movement of a single bird that appeared to be shadowing my fly.

Like saltwater game fish, many seabird species are highly migratory, generally moving north and inshore during the spring and south and offshore in the fall. Many species of birds follow the baitfish migration. Congregations of gulls, gannets, terns, or cormorants in our coastal waters signal the presence of baitfish. Active gulls, however, are the best indicators of game fish. Of the species mentioned above, gulls are the only ones that can't dive into the water and fish for themselves. They must rely on another predator for help. Clouds of tightly-packed screaming gulls low over the water indicate that bait is being driven to the surface. The size of the birds can often help you determine what the bait is. For example, diving terns usually feed on smaller baits such as sand eels, bay anchovy, and silversides, while gannets are much bigger and stronger and will feed on bigger baits like bunker and herring.

Moons and Tides

The moon probably has more influence on the success of saltwater fishing than any other element, yet it is often the most misunderstood piece of the puzzle. The phase of the moon controls tides, and tides deliver food to fish. Full moons and new moons provide for greater tidal exchange, with higher highs and lower lows. Generally, these conditions will improve the likelihood of success, as the greater fluctuations in tide mean stronger currents and more forage species being delivered helplessly by the currents to waiting predators.

False albacore are strong, powerful swimmers and take advantage of what Mother Nature has to offer during these heavy tidal exchanges. When fishing from shore, I like to work a narrow inlet, harbor mouth, or breachway during an incoming tide. False albacore are much more likely to come "inside" during a flooding tide. When the tide is outgoing, they tend to hang outside in the sound or ocean, feeding on bait that is being flushed out of the estuary. These fish are usually out of reach to the shorebound angler.

Knowing which moon phase brings an incoming tide to your favorite shore spot can be a critical decision in planning your fishing excursion. Some offshore rips fish well on both tides and shut down during the slack. Keep in mind, every hot spot has a happy hour, when the tidal current delivers the heaviest concentration of food. Once you have determined the happy hour of your hot spot, you can use tide charts to plan your trip. *The Eldridge Tide and Pilot Book* contains an annual tide chart for key areas from Maine to Florida. If you want to plan your trip before the next season's tide charts are available, it is easy to obtain calendars showing moon phases years in advance. For every moon phase, full or new, in every month, the tide is high at almost the exact same time at your favorite fishing location. You can count on this year after year. For example, at Menensha Inlet on Martha's Vineyard, the morning high on both the days of the new moon and full moon is between 8:00 and 9:00 AM. To fish the incoming tide from the inlet jetties, you could arrive at first light and fish the last of the incoming tide on both the new and full moon. Each day has two high tides and two low tides that occur on average six hours and twelve minutes apart. The times of the high and low tides advance by approximately 50 minutes every day. So, during the course of a week, the tides reverse themselves. Where it was high on the moon at 9:00 AM, one week after the moon it will be low, and in another week it will be high again at roughly 9:00 AM. Of course, the time of the tide varies greatly from location to location. But once you have established the time of high tide for your favorite hot spot on the day of the new and full moon, these times will hold true for every new and full moon, for every month and every year.

While I have been perfectly satisfied with my tide books for years, no tide book has room to list every location. You will still have to add or substract times to adjust for many locations, and longterm projections are difficult at best. Today there are computer software packages on the market that predict the tides out to the year 2100. I recently viewed one called *Tides & Currents for Windows* and was very excited about its potential as a planning tool for future fishing excursions.

The Fish Themselves

Albies are often very visible and noisy eaters, although they most frequently feed well below the surface. Surface swirls and splashes are obvious signs of fish, but you need to be able to distinguish between false albacore and other species from a distance. Striped bass usually create swirls and boils and push bait without much of a splash. Bluefish thrash, swirl, twist, and turn, with a lot of sloppy splashes. When you have violent, slicing eruptions with white-water sprays high in the air—resembling mortar shots—it's tuna time! While all three species are capable of going airborne during a blitz, it's much more common to see false albacore greyhounding, with heads and tails visible as they crash through schools of bait.

Tools of
the Trade

My fish was well into the backing when my partner hollered, "Fish on!" This would have been our fourth double on that Montauk morning. Then I heard a loud pop. At first, I thought it was a distant rifle shot, but as I spun around toward the stern, there was Ed Janiga, clinging to the butt half of his top-of-the-line graphite fly rod. We watched helplessly as the broken tip section sailed through the air in hot pursuit of his fly line until they both disappeared into the horizon.

This was not the first fly rod we have lost to false albacore, nor will it be the last. Broken rods and burned-out reels are common. Tuna are fast, tough, and aggressive fighting fish, and your tackle must be up to the challenge. Most guides fish for false albacore with the same outfits they use for tarpon in the 90-pound range. That is quite a tribute to the false albacore's fighting ability. Anglers who have not fished for false albacore often ask how these fish compare to another ocean speedster, the bonefish. Quite honestly, there is no comparison in terms of speed. As for power, I presented a hypothetical question to over two-dozen guides who have fished for both species. What would happen, I asked, if you tied the tails of a 10-pound bonefish and a 10-pound false albacore together? The only area of disagreement among the guides was how many seconds it would take for the bonefish to drown.

Rods

The rods commonly used to fish for false albacore range from 9- to 12-weight. Since false albacore fight like fish twice their size, you should play them just as aggressively to avoid a prolonged fight, thus ensuring a good survival rate after release. Anything lighter than a 9-weight won't allow you to do this. A good rule of thumb in fighting fish is that your line should always be moving: either the fish is taking line or you are. If you hook false albacore from a boat, they will usually continue to fight deep in the water column, even after they tire and are brought close to the boat. You need to have a rod with enough power to lift their heads as they circle below you. Graphite rods on the market today are much lighter and easier to cast than the bamboo and fiberglass rods that preceded them. My 10-weight graphite rod weighs less than my 6-weight classic bamboo trout rod. Although I have taken false albacore on rods from 8- to 12-weight in the Northeast, I prefer a 10-weight, and in North Carolina and Florida, where the fish generally run larger, I prefer an 11-weight outfit.

Today's multi-piece rods are so well made and durable that I strongly recommend 3- and 4-piece rods, especially for travel. They can be easily carried onto airplanes, and they fit into the overhead storage compartments. A traveling fisherman should never be separated from his fishing gear. Clothes and personal items are relatively easy to replace, but trying to replace lost fishing equipment can be difficult and very expensive and might ruin a great fishing trip.

Reels

The reel should also be of tarpon class. It needs to have the capacity to hold a full fly line and a minimum of 200 yards of 30-pound backing. False albacore are much stronger and faster than bonefish, and they don't burn energy on aerial displays like tarpon. They just bear down and slug it out like a heavyweight fighter. They swim fast enough to have any cork disk drag screaming for mercy. Blues and stripers are tough, but albies can smoke you. In addition to line capacity and a good drag system, you should consider the advantages a large-arbor reel has to offer. The first large-arbor reels that came on the market only increased the size of the arbor. When you increase the arbor size without increasing the diameter of the spool, you just decrease the volume of backing and have done nothing to increase the speed of line retrieval. Modern large-arbor reels increase both the size of the arbor and the diameter of the spool. This design enables you to pick up more line per revolution than traditionally-sized arbors, thereby increasing the speed of line retrieval.

After albies take a fly and make their initial run, they often turn and

DAVE W. SKOK

At speeds of up to 40 mph, false albacore can have any cork disk drag screaming for mercy.

come back to you, throwing slack in the line. A large-arbor reel can help you gather slack more efficiently and keep constant pressure on the fish. The choice between direct-drag and anti-reverse models is a matter of personal preference. I prefer the old standby and most commonly used direct-drive models. The handle is attached directly to the spool, and basically, the spool does what you and the handle tell it to. In general, direct-drives are easier to clean and maintain, and I like having the option of adjusting the pressure I put on the fish by palming the exposed spool.

The only downside to direct-drive reels is that until you get used to an albie's speed, you might have your knuckles whacked by the handle. This could be cause for concern for certain professionals, like doctors and dentists, whose patients might not appreciate their battle-scarred hands. In this case, I would recommend the anti-reverse models. When a fish takes line from an anti-reverse reel, the handle remains in position. Recently, manufacturers have been making anti-reverse reels with exposed spools. This allows the angler to apply additional pressure by palming the spool, a nice feature that was not available on earlier models.

Fly Lines

Today, we are both blessed and cursed with a tremendous assortment of fly lines. Blessed because there is a line to cover virtually every fishing situation, and cursed because there are so many lines to choose from that it can be difficult for anglers to select the right one. Modern saltwater lines have a weight-forward design that features a relatively short, thick, heavy, front or "head," followed by a long, thin running or shooting line. These weight-forward lines load the rod with less line in the air than traditional tapers. Most saltwater tapers on the market today have a weight-forward head of 30 to 38 feet. The Striper Line from Scientific Anglers, for example, has a 38-foot head, while their Mastery Series Distance Taper has a 59-foot head. The Distance Taper line casts very well, but the drawback is that you must have most of the head in the air to load the rod, and that requires more false casts. When chasing false albacore, you want to make quick casts with a minimum of false casts, preferably only one. A weight-forward fly line with a relatively short head is the ticket.

I have taken false albacore on floating, intermediate, and sinking lines, as well as shooting heads and combinations of each. They all can have their day. Selection is really dictated by personal preference as much as fishing conditions. I would suggest that you not limit yourself to just one line. In fact, I wouldn't venture out after albacore without at least one backup rod, reel, and line.

When possible, I like to have the visual thrill of having the fish attack my offering at or near the surface, so my first line of choice is an intermediate sinking line. This line has neutral density and sinks slowly at about 1.5 inches per second. There are several advantages to fishing this type of line. Its diameter is thinner than that of a floating line so it will handle better in windy conditions. Intermediate lines also fish just under the surface "clutter" and wave action, giving you good control over your fly. Because they stay close to the surface, intermediates are much easier to pick up and cast than a faster-sinking line. In a pinch, you can even fish topwater sliders and poppers with an intermediate line.

Back in the mid-1990s, I had the opportunity to participate in Scientific Anglers' Goodwill Ambassador program. There were a dozen "ambassadors" from around the country, and our job was to give angler education programs and seminars in our respective regions. This ambassadorship provided me the opportunity to field-test their fly lines, and it was during this time that I discovered their Stillwater line, the first truly clear line that I had fished. It was designed for fishing for trout in clear lakes and ponds, and I thought it might be a good line for chasing bonito. The Stillwater line cast well and was nearly invisible in the water, but it had two drawbacks for chasing tuna. It was not available above a 9-weight, and it had a long head, which required several false casts to have enough line out to load the rod. False casts are fine for cruising trout, but not for blitzing tuna. Today, several manufacturers make clear or translucent intermediate fly lines, with short, weight-forward heads. These lines don't spook the fish and allow you to fish shorter leaders, which can make it easier to turn over a bulky or weighted fly.

My second line of choice would be a sinking line. When fishing from a boat, if fish are not showing or when fishing offshore rips, I start by searching deep with a fast-sinking line. Rather than a full-sinking line, I prefer a line with a fast-sinking head of about 30 to 38 feet, followed by a thin running line that is either floating or intermediate. When I first started chasing albies, I used a 30-foot Cortland sinking, shooting head, and a loop-to-loop connection to attach the head to a thin running line. I used the rear level sections of an old weight-forward floating trout line or 30-pound braided mono as the running line. These lines would cast much farther than full-sink lines because the shooting head pulled the very light running line effortlessly through the rod's guides.

While there were sinking lines on the market back in the early 1960s, they were coated with lead and their sink rates were slow. Scientific Anglers developed a fast-sinking line using powered tungsten. Jim Teeny worked with them to develop his Teeny Series, which came on the market in 1983. His one-piece design, with a fast-sinking head and a smooth transition into a thin running line, virtually eliminated the need to cut and splice shooting heads and running lines. Although heads still have practical applications, they take up a less prominent position in my line collection. Jim initially designed his lines for steelhead fishing, and they were a little short for saltwater application. My first Teeny line was the T-300; it was 84 feet long with a 24-foot, fast-sinking head. Despite coming up a little short in both the head and overall length, it served me well in the salt for a number of years.

As more coastal anglers used the Teeny lines, Jim developed the Saltwater Series in 1993, lengthening the head to 30 feet and the line length to 100 feet. The Freshwater Teeny lines are numbered in even 100s (T-200, T-300, T-400) and the new Saltwater lines are 50s (T-250, T-350, T-450). The number corresponds to the weight in grams of the first 30 feet of fly line. For example, the first 30 feet of a Teeny 350 weighs 350 grams. A rod's line rating is related to the weight in grams per foot of fly line. A 10-weight rod is designed to fish a line that weighs 10 grams per foot. A Teeny 350 weighs a little over 11 grams per foot (350 grams / 30 feet = 11⅔). It loads both a 10- and 11-weight rod well.

Soon, other line manufacturers began developing lines with quick-sinking heads and thinner, lighter running lines. I have had good results with Cortland's Quick Descent, Orvis' Depth Charge, RIO's Density Compensated Sink Tip, and Air Flo's Depth Finder, which also has a density compensated front taper. The newer designs on the market have eliminated the "hinge effect" by having a thicker floating or intermediate section following the sinking head that gradually tapers into the thin running line. This makes false casting easier and smoother and the lines more durable. When fishing in extremely windy conditions, you may have trouble keeping these thin running lines from blowing out of a stripping basket. During these conditions a full-sinking line may be the only line you can cast efficiently. The extra weight of the running line will also hold it in a basket or on a boat deck.

Floating lines allow for quicker pickups and casts to moving fish, but due to their thickness they don't cast as well into the wind. Orvis was the first to market "ghost tip" lines, a floating line with a 10-foot, clear, intermediate tip. This gives you easy pickup for casting, and because the tip is clear, you can fish a short leader without spooking the fish. This line can be especially effective on calm, clear days when fish are being picky.

Leaders and Tippet

Every guide and albie fanatic I have fished with has different theories on tackle and techniques. At the mention of leaders there will be heated debates as to length, strength, and the use of fluorocarbon tippets. Over the years, I have seen hundreds of albies taken on leaders of less than 7 feet and tippets testing over 20 pounds. Guides repeatedly report landing albies on wire and heavy shock tippet. I think a lot depends on the type of water you are fishing and how the fish are feeding. In calm, clear water with little or no current, your choice of fly line and leader is more critical than when you're fishing in fast current or in off-colored water. On calm, clear days, I like to fish a clear fly line and a 7- to 9-foot leader with a tippet of 12-pound test. If my fly line were not clear, I would fish a leader of 9 to 12 feet, again with a 12-pound tippet. When fishing in fast current, I increase my tippet strength to 15 to 20 pounds. When fishing a sinking line and weighted fly, I generally fish a very short leader of 5 feet or less so that the fly line and the fly are at about the same depth. This increases my chances of feeling the take and hooking up.

As for tippet material, nothing can get you into an argument faster than asking the question: monofilament or fluorocarbon? The refractive index of fluorocarbon is almost identical to that of water, making it nearly invisible. It is denser and, therefore, sinks faster than monofilament, and it is more resistant to abrasion. When the first generation of fluorocarbon leader materials came on the scene, many fishermen had problems with their knots breaking. Today, this is much less of a problem, and more and more guides are switching to fluorocarbon tippets when false albacore get finicky. They claim it often makes a difference. Of the guides I interviewed, fluorocarbon was preferred over monofilament by a margin of two to one. The guides who fish the clear waters of the Northeast choose fluorocarbon by a margin of four to one. In North Carolina, where there are often vast schools of both bait and predators, it's a toss up.

Off the east coast of Florida, where guides almost exclusively use live chum to drum up false albacore, the use of fluorocarbon is rare and considered by most to be a waste of money. Capt. Scott Hoffmister, who for years has been chumming false albacore into frenzies for his clients, claims to have had albies take pilchards right off his gaff. And when he wants a few albies to use as bait for blue marlin, he says, "I just put a hooked pilchard on 10 feet of 300-pound mono, tie it to a boat cleat, toss it into the frenzy and let those sons of bitches hang themselves."

I think Capt. Dave Chouinard, owner of The Fly Hatch in Red Bank, New Jersey, framed this debate best when he said he "had questioned two albies on the need for fluorocarbon, and one albie said it didn't matter and the other said it did." Chouinard went on to say that in his home waters, he doesn't get the number of albies that locations like Montauk Point, New York, and Harkers Island, North Carolina do. His season is shorter, so he feels that anything he can do that might give him an edge is worth trying.

What has convinced me to add fluorocarbon to my tackle bag is the fact that, despite its relatively high cost, it's now widely used by commercial tuna fishermen who depend on their success to earn a living.

Knots

Because of the false albacore's blinding speed, I prefer my backing and fly line to be joined with knotless loop-to-loop connections. On more than one occasion, I have seen a knot jam into a fly-rod guide and break off the fish, the guide, or even the rod itself. Interlocking loops can fly through the guides at great speeds with little or no chance of hanging up.

Backing Knots

A "no-knot" backing splice, or "blind" splice, makes the perfect loop in Dacron backing. Dacron is hollow, which enables you to splice the tag end of the Dacron back through itself, forming a knotless loop. While I have made this splice with 20-pound backing, it's much easier on backing of 30 pounds and above. In addition to being easier to splice, 30-pound backing allows you to fish heavier tippets, and it packs better on the spool, with less chance of binding than 20-pound. You will need a piece of thin, single-strand, stainless steel wire to make the splice. I recommend a 16-inch piece of number 2 or 3 trolling wire.

1. Fold the wire in half and pinch the fold to a point. For ease of changing lines, you'll want the loop to be large enough to slip over a reel or fly line spool.

Bend wire

2. Insert the wire about two feet above the tag end of the backing.
3. Insert the point end of the wire into the hollow core and work the wire for 4 to 6 inches toward the tag end of the backing. Once you have the wire inside the Dacron for the desired distance, push it outside the braid.

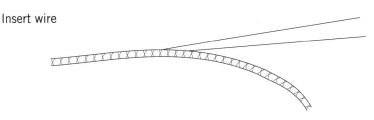

Insert wire

4. Insert the tag end of the Dacron into the loop on the wire and pull it out the other side about an inch.

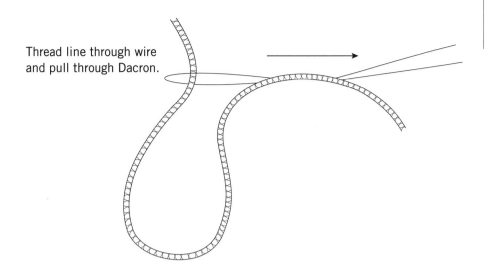

Thread line through wire and pull through Dacron.

5. Hold the two tag ends of the wire and pull the tag end of the Dacron back inside and through the core of the Dacron. Continue pulling until the wire and tag end of the line exit the core. Now you can adjust the size of the loop by gently pulling on the tag to shorten the loop or on the loop end to increase the loop's size.

6. You can now tighten the loop by pulling on it with one hand and the standing line with the other. This forces the hollow core to squeeze down and tighten, like a Chinese finger puzzle. While this is a very dependable knot, I like to add a second splice about an inch above the first by repeating steps two through five.

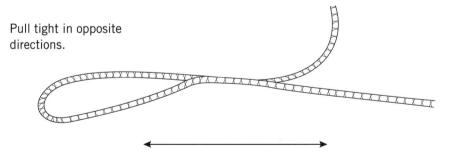

Pull tight in opposite directions.

7. Trim the tag end of the second splice so that it ends inside the core of the second splice.

8. Apply a small amount of flexible glue for about ½ inch at the tag end of the rear splice.

Fly-Line Knots

I use a whipped loop at both ends of my fly line. Properly tied, this knot will never break or catch on the guides.

1. Taper the tip of the fly line by cutting it on a 45-degree angle with a safety razor blade.
2. Fold the fly line back about three-quarters of an inch.
3. Take a bobbin and wrap the thread about three times around one leg to increase tension. Make several wraps around the two sides of the folded loop in the fly line.

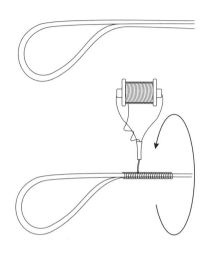

4. Now swing the bobbin around the loop. The faster the swing the more the thread will bite into the fly line and secure the knot. Wrap until you have only about a quarter-inch loop left in the fly line.

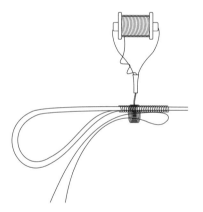

5. To finish the knot, take a short piece of 8-pound mono and form a loop. Lay this against the whipped loop and make eight or nine wraps over the mono against the whipped section of the loop. Cut the thread and slip it through the mono loop. Pull both tag ends of the mono, thus pulling the end of the thread under the wraps.

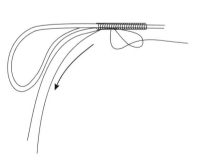

6. Coat with flexible cement like Pliobond.

Leader and Tippet Knots

For leaders and tippets, I like to keep my knots simple so that they can be tied with confidence under the most difficult conditions. The following knots have served me well and can be tied in the face of wind, rain, low light, and even blitzing fish.

Interlocking Loop-to-Loop Connection

To connect the butt of the leader to the fly line, I use an interlocking loop-to-loop connection. Connect the fly line's whipped looped to the butt end of the leader with a surgeon's loop.

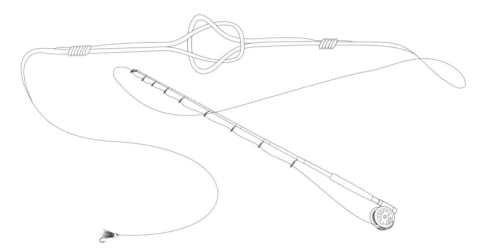

Surgeon's Loop

The surgeon's loop is a very easy knot to tie and has a 90 percent breaking strength, which is more than adequate, as the butt section of your leader should be tied with at least 30-pound mono.

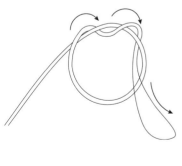

1. Form a loop in the butt section of the leader, and tie an overhand knot.
2. Tie a second overhand knot.
3. Wet the knot and pull all four tag ends evenly until the knot is tight.
4. Cut the tag end.

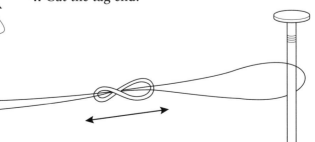

Surgeon's Knot

A surgeon's knot is similar to the surgeon's loop. It's very simple to tie and when tied properly it doesn't slip, even when using leaders of different diameter or strength. It's my first choice for tying the tippet section to the leader.

1. Place the leader and tippet parallel and overlap for about 12 inches.

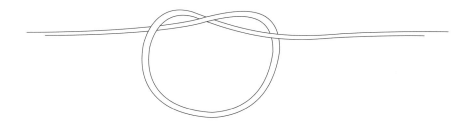

2. Tie an overhand knot, pulling the entire tippet through the loop.

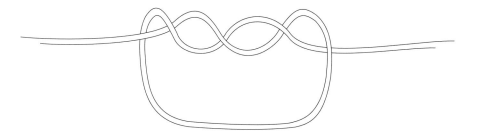

3. Tie a second overhand knot.

4. Wet the knot and pull all four tag ends evenly until the knot is tight.
5. Trim the tag ends.

Cut   Cut

Non-Slip Mono Loop

The non-slip mono loop, while more difficult than some knots that are used to tie on the fly, is certainly worth the time to master. It has excellent knot strength and it lets small flies "swim" no matter how heavy a tippet you use.

1. Tie a loose overhand knot about 6 to 8 inches from the tag end of the tippet.
2. Run the end of the tippet through the hook eye and back through the overhand knot.
3. Wrap the tag end around the standing line and take it back through the overhand knot as if you were tying a clinch knot.
4. Wet knot and uniformly tighten.

Stripping Baskets

Stripping baskets are a must for shore-bound anglers. They store the line safely away from weeds, rocks, and wave action that can impair your casts and tangle your line.

Baskets can be a big help for boat fishermen, as well. I can't count the number of times I have botched a cast or lost a fish because the wind blew my line around some obstacle in the boat. Wind and wave action can easily put the line under your feet or around gear bags or spare rods stored horizontally below the gunwale. Offshore winds can actually blow thin running line right out of the boat. All of these perils can be reduced, if not eliminated, with the use of a stripping basket. If you run the boat to breaking fish, a basket can safely hold the line tangle-free so you'll be ready to cast the moment you reach the fish. When the action is hot and

DAVE W. SKOK

George Ryan fighting an albie at the Hook of Cape Lookout, North Carolina

heavy and one angler hooks up, a second angler wearing a basket can still continue to fish without getting in the way of the angler fighting the fish.

Baskets come in all sizes, shapes, and designs. While there are some very lightweight, collapsible models on the market, I prefer the hard plastic, "dishpan" basket. I like two sizes, a shallow basket for deep wading and a deep basket for jetties and boat fishing. The shallow basket lets me wade a little deeper and, therefore, farther out when casting from the beach. When I'm not wading, the deeper basket helps prevent wind from blowing line out of the basket. I am not a big proponent of putting holes in my baskets to let water out; this is especially problematic when you wade deep. The holes will let water in and your line will develop tangles. Holes (and lots of them) are a must, however, when fishing in big surf or in heavy rain.

In addition to size, another important element to consider is how you attach the basket to your waist. A wide belt is a much better choice than a bungy cord. The best system is to have the belt slide through slots on each side of the back of the basket. When you hook a fish, the basket can be pushed to the side and around the back, giving you freedom to fight the fish. It's also a good idea to keep the basket behind you when walking rocky shorelines and jetties so that you can see your footing. The inside bottom of the basket should have some device to prevent your line from moving around and tangling. Most baskets have stiff monofilament lawn-trimmer line or cone inserts. If you are making your own basket using stiff mono, it's best to double the mono over. Single strands tend to curl over time and can hook your line as it shoots out. Forgetting a basket can ruin a fishing trip, so the first thing I pack, even when flying, is my stripping basket. It can fit neatly in a corner of my carry-on bag. Then I place my reels and fly boxes inside it, being careful not to bend the mono line-control devices.

Carrying Your Gear

Shore fishermen have three good options for transporting gear: a vest, a chest pack, or a shoulder bag. Having fished for trout for almost 40 years, I realize old habits are hard to break. I generally prefer to carry my gear in a shortie vest. A good vest has many advantages, but the biggest one is that there is a pocket specially designed for everything you'll need. My fishing closet has two loaded shortie vests, one packed for trout streams and another ready for a day at the beach. My vests have pockets for sunglasses, sunscreen, bug juice, flashlight, pliers, leaders, tippet material, several fly boxes, and a small 35mm waterproof camera. There is plenty of rear storage for raingear and even a sandwich and beverage. The vest serves me well along jetties, inlets, and estuaries where wave action is minimal.

When fishing the good wave action of the open ocean, however, I prefer a chest pack instead of a vest to keep my gear high and dry. Several manufacturers have designed these packs with the salty flyrodder in mind. If you choose to fish with a chest pack, make sure that it is one with large pockets, both front and rear. In the front, I like to carry two fly boxes, tippet material, and a small camera. In the rear, I carry raingear, water, and extra tackle.

Another option that works well from the beach and boat is a shoulder bag. From shore, you'll want a bag to be small and light enough that you will not be tempted to put it down on the beach. You always want to be mobile without having to go back for your bag or worrying about an incoming tide washing your equipment away. A 6x6x12-inch bag is large enough to carry several fly boxes, an extra reel, a camera, pliers, and leader and tippet material. The better models can also store raingear either on the side or under the bottom of the bag.

Something happens to anglers when they prepare to fish from a boat. Gear-mania takes over and they tend to pack everything they own. Most inshore fly fishing boats are 18- to 21-foot center consoles with minimal storage areas. What little storage area that is available is not readily accessible when the fishing heats up. This is especially true when your boat and camera bags are so large that the captain's only option is to stow them in the bow storage area. Reaching this gear is particularly problematic when your fishing partner is standing on the bow hatch fighting a fish.

My favorite gear bag for boat fishing is an Able Bag. It holds everything that I'll need on a trip and it makes a perfect airline carry-on bag. It's a little large to have on the deck of a small boat, though. A better choice in this situation is a small shoulder bag. It takes up so little space that it doesn't have to be stored out of sight. As I am a tackle junky, I board with two bags. One is a small bag with sunscreen, a small waterproof camera, and my immediate fishing tools that can be stored on deck. The other is a larger bag that holds extra gear and clothes that can be stored out of the way.

High and Dry

Nothing can ruin a day on the water like getting cold and wet. The selection of proper boots and outerwear is critical to a successful and enjoyable fishing trip. For coastal anglers, stocking-foot waders are a poor choice for several reasons, including the fact that sand can get inside the shoe, gaiter zippers corrode and jam, and eyelets on boots eventually rust. Boot-foot waders are the best choice and, unless you fish only sand beaches, you'll want felt soles on the bottom of your boots. When fishing jetties or rocky areas, it is a good investment in your safety to have a set of cleats or corkers that can be slipped on over your boots.

There are several types of waders available. I prefer waders that are light enough to walk the beaches in summer without getting overheated. As the season cools, I add long johns under my fishing pants for comfort. If your budget allows, consider purchasing two pairs: lightweight and breathable for summer and neoprene for the colder months.

The other critical item in keeping dry is raingear. The coastal angler must defend against the effects of rain, morning dew, and salt spray in boats and wave action on the beach. You want your rain jacket to be long enough to fit below your waist. Wear it over your waders so that water from waves and rain run down over your boots. For added safety and comfort, cinch your rain jacket snug around your waist with a wader belt. I prefer elastic cuffs rather than Velcro straps; elastic cuffs are tight, which helps keep water from running up your sleeve. Velcro is not good at keeping water out, and the straps have a tendency to catch your fly line.

Documenting Your Catch

With the increase in catch-and-release fishing, many anglers are carrying cameras to memorialize their catch. If you want to take quality photos and minimize the amount of time the fish is out of the water, you need to prepare ahead. The photographer should have the camera ready and the shot planned before the fish is landed. How many times have we seen others, or been guilty ourselves, of landing a fish and then deciding to take a photo? If you have to hunt through your gear bag, then hand your camera to a partner, and then instruct them on how to use it, just don't take the shot. In these circumstances, you're most likely going to be disappointed with your photo, and even worse, you will have put the fish at risk.

I have been fortunate over the last 30 years to have Ed Jaworowski as one of my mentors and close friends. In addition to being a world-class fly caster, instructor, and outdoor writer, Ed is also a professional photographer. My den walls are filled with great shots of fish, courtesy of Ed's talent and generosity.

If you are not lucky enough to have your own "cameraman," plan the photos you want well in advance. Start with a full roll of film in the camera. Instruct your partner on how to use your camera before you begin fishing. Keep your camera in a dry, accessible location. When a fish is hooked, discuss with your fellow anglers the positions you want them in when the fish is landed. Also, consider the location of the sun and the background you want in the photo.

I pack two cameras. The one I use most frequently is a small, fixed-lens, point-and-shoot waterproof camera. It gets a lot of use because it's convenient. It fits easily into my vest, raincoat, or small boat bag and is always accessible. I strongly recommend that your camera be waterproof, so you will be able to carry it on every fishing excursion.

My second camera has a macro lens for close-ups of fish, baitfish, and flies. Photo-documenting baitfish aids greatly in my effort to match local baits at the tying bench. You should consider having a polarized filter to reduce sun glare and its reflection off the water, as well as a fill flash, which provides additional light when necessary to eliminate shadows. Good photographs don't just happen; they are planned. You will have treasured photos and still safely release your prize to fight another day.

Fishing Log

Fly fishing, for most anglers, is 90 percent preparation, anticipation, and memories and 10 percent time on the water. With so little actual fishing time, I try to enjoy some aspect of my sport almost daily. It may be reading the latest fly-fishing magazine, watching Saturday morning fishing programs, tying flies, or looking through my photo albums. I enjoy the anticipation and preparation for my next trip or the memories of my most recent outing. One tool that has helped increase the enjoyment and productivity of my fishing is my fishing log. I have kept a log for over 30 years, recording the details of catching over 10,000 game fish. It is a wonderful way to remember your days on the water, and it helps unlock many of nature's secrets. A log permanently records your catch while it is still fresh in your mind, so that you can document all the variables that went into your day on the water. Some basic information that can provide valuable clues toward future success include the stage of the tide that was most productive, water temperature, moon phase, the bait the fish were feeding on, wind direction, general weather conditions, and the flies that were most and least productive. If possible, at the end of a fishing day (or night) you should make some rough notes while everything is still fresh in your mind. Later, you can expand on this information to describe fish behavior, presentations that worked, and the tackle used, especially lines. In the off-season, I spend many enjoyable hours pouring over my logs, remembering good times on the water. I am also looking for answers and identifying patterns or trends.

Important
East Coast Baitfish

I'll never forget the first mayfly hatch I witnessed. I had been fishing a small trout stream in northeastern Pennsylvania for several hours with little success. I was totally unprepared for the spectacle Mother Nature was about to unveil. My first clue that something magical was about to occur was the sudden appearance of dozens of swallows flying low over the water. Having fished one small pool for about twenty minutes without any action, I was about to move upstream when I noticed a small gray butterfly-like insect floating on the surface of the water. It struggled as it was pulled down the pool by the current. Then there was a sudden splash and the small creature was gone.

Several more of these little insects started to appear, often vanishing in a sudden splash. Within minutes, dozens of trout were feeding in a pool I had thought devoid of life. I decided to join in the action and catch some of these trout that were now feeding without caution. Cast after cast, fly after fly, my offerings were ignored as the fish continued to feed. The birds, insects, and trout all participated in this performance, but my ignorance excluded me. This experience made me very determined to learn how to become a player. Before I left the stream that April afternoon, I collected some samples of the insects that were being consumed in great quantities by the swallows and brook trout.

That evening, I pulled out my copy of the book *Match the Hatch*, by Ernest Schwiebert, which was my first fly-fishing book and a Christmas gift from my wife, Joanne. I had attempted to read it several times earlier that spring, but every time I started, Schwiebert would hurl out a few un-

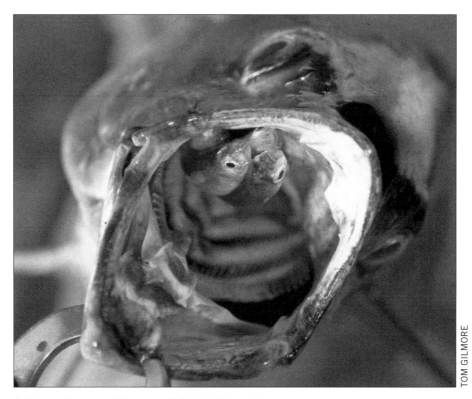

A false albacore with a mouthful of silversides

familiar Latin names, and I would put it down in frustration. But that night things were different. Armed with my streamside observations and samples of the insects that were hatching, *Match the Hatch* now had real meaning for me. It didn't take long to identify the little mayfly I had captured and to decipher what I had observed on the water. This insect was known by the Latin name *Paraleptophlebia adoptiva* and was commonly called an Iron Blue Dun, Little Dun, or Blue Quill.

Schwiebert went on to explain that this diminutive species is one of the earliest mayflies to appear on Eastern trout waters, hatching from the third week in April through the middle of May. They would begin emerging around eleven o'clock in the morning and continue most of the day. The spectacle that I observed was not random, but a predictable annual occurrence.

I didn't have the opportunity to meet *Paraleptophlebia adoptiva* again until the following spring. I returned to that same trout stream in late April armed with a dozen Blue Quill dry flies. By late that morning, swallows were flying low over the water picking off diminutive blue-gray mayflies that were being delivered downcurrent to hungry trout. Before the day was over a dozen or more beautiful native trout took my fly as if it were the real thing. This time I was a player. I began to understand what fly fishing was really about. I felt I was at one with nature, and life was good. As my knowledge of stream entomology improved, so did my fishing success and enjoyment.

I often fished for bass, pickerel, flounder, and bluefish, but I felt nothing could ever match my love for the challenges and discoveries that "match-the-hatch" trout fishing provided. In the early 1980s, I often joined my fishing club on its annual bluefish trip to Martha's Vineyard. Tossing metal lures and surface poppers into the surf with 10-foot spinning rods, we did catch our share of feisty bluefish. Occasionally, these fish would come close enough to reach with a fly rod. A gaudy streamer or noisy popper would usually do the trick. I enjoyed the size and strength of these fish, but I felt that catching them was due more to luck than skill. I missed the challenge that trout fishing provided.

On my third trip to the Vineyard, we heard reports of a few striped bass being caught at Lobsterville Beach. This was still the early 1980s, and striper stocks were very low. As a teenager, I remembered reading about Joe Brooks catching a world-record 29-pound striper on a skipping bug, and I had always wanted to catch one of these magnificent creatures on a fly. So I fished Lobsterville every night for several hours, and while I did catch several nice blues, it wasn't until the wee hours of the morning on our last day that I landed my first striped bass. It was only a "schoolie," but it was still a fly-caught bass. At that time, landing any striper on a fly was a real accomplishment; however, it was the fish that I couldn't catch that morning that captivated me.

At first light, I witnessed at least one hundred bass boiling within casting distance, feeding on what turned out to be sand eels. For about a half-hour, I made cast after cast without a touch. Just like on that trout stream a dozen years before, I was surrounded by nature but not part of it. I would later discover that sand eels enter the shallows along Lobsterville Beach at dusk and burrow into the sand for safety. They then emerge from the shallows next to the beach at first light to be greeted by striped bass feeding like piranhas. Like the blue quill hatch, the sand eel emergence was a predictable annual occurrence. I now return to this beach each year on the new moon in June. Under the security of the dark moon, stripers feed without caution, and I participate as an active player in nature's feeding frenzy.

Sand eel and herring

A good trout fisherman has to develop knowledge and skills such as reading the water, understanding feeding positions, and identifying rise forms. I had always thought that saltwater fishing was mostly "chuck and duck." I didn't realize that tidal flows and moon phases could trigger hatches equivalent to those in a trout stream. Those sand eels emerging at dawn or the mating swarms of aquatic worms or shrimp bring about heavy feeding and are predictable events. I began to discover that the ocean and its fish could provide all the challenges a fly fisherman might ever want. The fish and their food supply are migratory, and water levels and currents change with every tick of the clock. Understanding the marine environment and the baitfish and their habits are necessary ingredients for success and will enhance the enjoyment of this great sport.

Bass, bonito, false albacore, and at times even bluefish can be selective feeders. A working knowledge of your region's baitfish, along with their migration patterns, will greatly improve your angling success. You should know when the baitfish will arrive and depart, their preferred habitat, and when they are most vulnerable to predators. Study how they swim and their dominant body features, such as length, shape, color, and amount of flash. This information will improve your ability to match the baitfish in your fly selection and presentation.

False albacore have relatively small mouths and little in the way of teeth. They must take the bait whole; therefore, they generally favor small baits. Let's take a closer look at some of the more significant East Coast baitfish that false albacore target.

American Sand Lance (*Ammodytes americanus*)

American sand lances, or sand eels as they are more frequently called, are a very abundant and important inshore baitfish in the Northeast. They are found from the Gulf of St. Lawrence south to Cape Hatteras. Sand eels are not actually members of the eel family; they are very slender bait-fish with long, pointed heads. Their long slender bodies—approximately 12 times as long as they are wide—make them easy to imitate with a fly. Most of the sand eels I see range from one to three years of age and average between 2 and 4 inches in length. However, they can live up to nine years, and I have seen them as large as 8 inches. Sand eels are olive to brown on top with pearly white underbellies. Their eyes are small and yellowish with a black pupil. Sand eels are known for their burrowing abilities and are generally found over sandy bottoms. When they are resting or threatened, they will dig into the sand or mud to escape preda-tors. They burrow into the sand at night and rise at dawn, often pro-viding first-light blitzes close to shore. They spawn from November until March, and usually arrive in our estuaries in late May or early June and stay into November.

Bay Anchovy (*Anchoa mitchilli*)

Bay anchovies, known locally as whitebait, rain fish, or glass minnows, are another important East Coast baitfish. They range from Cape Cod to Florida, with the greatest concentrations found from Rhode Island south to North Carolina. They migrate into Northeast coastal waters from Sep-tember through mid-October. On the Outer Banks of North Carolina, they leave the vast sounds along with silversides as the water cools in late October and early November. In both regions, the bay anchovy migration usually coincides with the peak of the false albacore run.

Juveniles can run under an inch, while adults can reach 3 to 4 inches in size. In the autumn, along the inshore waters in the Northeast, bay an-chovy generally run as small as 1 to 1½ inches. Along the Outer Banks, it

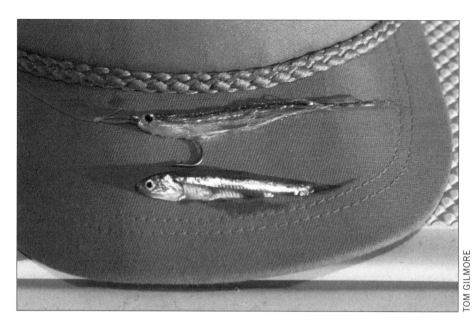

Bay anchovy and Mushmouth

is common to see them in the 3- to 4-inch range. What they lack in size, they make up for in numbers. I was once driven out of the surf by a 20-foot-long, 3-foot-wide brown object that was slowly swimming toward me in about 3 feet of water. The object, which I mistook for a shark, turned out to be a huge school of tightly-packed bay anchovies. When they are swimming at the surface in these vast schools, they cause the water to appear "nervous," almost like a light rain shower—hence the nickname "rain fish."

The backs of bay anchovies are yellowish brown and their bodies are translucent, with a white belly and a hint of a silver lateral line. Their eyes are large compared to the overall size of the fish, and I believe the eye is a very important detail on imitations. Fish feeding on bay anchovies often appear to be very selective and present a greater challenge for the angler. I have discovered that there are two reasons for this. First, just the sheer numbers of bait make it hard for your offering to be singled out. Second, anglers often overlook the bay anchovy's diminutive size. It's rare for saltwater fly fishermen to have patterns in their arsenal as small as 1 to 1½ inches, and when fish are feeding heavily on small bay anchovies, they usually ignore larger offerings.

While I originally learned to tie traditional trout flies using only natural materials, I have found that many of the new synthetics on the market are not only more durable but often more realistic in appearance, especially when trying to achieve the translucent, almost transparent, look that so many of our baitfish possess. This is particularly true for bay anchovy and silversides.

Atlantic Silverside (*Menidia menidia*)

Atlantic silversides, known locally as spearing, glass minnows, or shiners, are perhaps the East Coast's most abundant inshore baitfish. Their range is from the Gulf of St. Lawrence in the north down to the Gulf of Mexico. Silversides are short-lived, with only a small percentage reaching two years of age. They are sexually mature at one year, and most die after completing their first spawn. I have seen silversides as large as 5 or 6 inches, but the average is about 3 to 4 inches. Silversides are easy to distinguish from other baits in the water, as they will playfully jump over a small piece of floating debris or a floating fly line. They have olive-green backs, a very distinguishable silver lateral line, and a pearlescent white translucent belly. Similar to the bay anchovy, their eye is a very dominant feature and should be incorporated into imitations.

While they are schooling fish, silversides do not form as dense a school as do sand eels, bunker, or bay anchovy. This trait will often make tuna feeding on silversides easier to catch. Capt. Tim Flarity, one of the top guides on Martha's Vineyard, was the first to point this out to me. My fishing partner and I had spent several days with Tim, chasing false alba-

Silverside and Surf Candy

TOM GILMORE

core that were crashing through dense schools of "peanut" bunker. Getting the fish to take our flies was extremely difficult. I probably had more good shots rejected in these few days than I normally do in an entire season. We tried every conceivable combination of fly line, leader, tippet, and flies. While we did have limited success, it paled in comparison to the numerous opportunities we had. We concluded that there was just too much bait in the water.

As we rounded West Chop one afternoon on the way back to Vineyard Haven, we spotted a small pod of fish chasing bait. Our first casts brought a double hook-up. We thought we were into bluefish, but the fish ran like tuna. As it turned out, we were surrounded by bonito. My fishing partner and I hooked back-to-back doubles and released five fish in just over 30 minutes before the action subsided. Why were these normally finicky bonito almost suicidal in the way they were devouring our flies? Flarity pointed out a small school of silversides and told us that when tuna are feeding on them, they are often easier to catch because silversides school close to the water's surface, making feeding tuna more visible to anglers. Your flies can also be seen more readily in the less dense schools.

Atlantic Menhaden (*Brevoortia tyrannus*)

Menhaden are the most commercially important fish in the United States. Their availability as forage fish has varied greatly over the last few decades, depending on harvest regulations. Adult menhaden, also called bunker or pogie, present too big a mouthful for false albacore, but the young of the year can be very important forage fish for inshore tuna. In recent years, there have been vast amounts of juvenile bunker in Northeast waters from New Jersey to Cape Cod. More and more anglers are making patterns imitating the young of the year, known as peanut bunker, part of their arsenal. Menhaden range from the northern Gulf of St. Lawrence to Jupiter Inlet in South Florida. Gulf menhaden (*Brevoortia patronus*) are similar in appearance to Atlantic menhaden and are found in southern Florida and the Gulf of Mexico. Menhaden are usually easy to spot because they swim in massive schools near the surface, causing a slight ripple. When menhaden are in large, densely-packed schools, fishing can be very challenging. I often have better success presenting my fly just outside or below the school of bait.

Young of the year spend their first six months of life in estuaries. When they begin to leave these estuaries in massive schools on their autumn journey to wintering grounds in the South Atlantic, fishing can be

TOM GILMORE

Juvenile peanut bunker with Clouser Minnow and Hamilton Special

unbelievable, with schools of striped bass, bluefish, bonito, and false albacore all feeding on menhaden in the mouths of these estuaries.

Striped Mullet (*Mugil cephalus*)

Striped mullet range from Cape Cod, Massachusetts to the tropical waters of South America. They can be a very important early fall migrant along the East Coast and are especially popular with anglers in New York, New Jersey, and on the east coast of Florida. They often can be seen swimming near the surface of the water, creating the aforementioned "nervous water." During their southerly journey, they hug the beaches to avoid predators that follow their migration. This brings blitzing predators chasing mullet right to the beach, a combination that is a coastal fly fisherman's dream. Mullet in the Northeast most often average 4 to 5 inches in length. They are round in shape and medium-bodied, with silvery-white sides and dark blue-gray backs. Their eyes are prominent and appear to bulge out, again making the eyes an important part of any imitation.

Immature butterfish (right), herring (bottom), and fly

Butterfish (*Peprilus triancanthus*)

Butterfish range from Nova Scotia south to the Carolinas. They tend to migrate into northern harbors and estuaries in late summer through early autumn. On more than one occasion, I have seen false albacore actually come in under boat docks to chase butterfish that have schooled there for protection from predators. This is a relatively common occurrence at the town dock in Edgartown on Martha's Vineyard, where locals use treble hooks to snag butterfish and then live-line them very successfully for false albacore. Butterfish are a very wide-bodied, almost oval-shaped, fish that can grow up to a foot in length. The juvenile fish, from 2 to 4 inches, are often on the menu of false albacore. Butterfish have a silvery, blue-green back, with silver sides and a silver belly. Their large eyes are very prominent and will be a vital component of any realistic imitation.

Striped Anchovy (*Anchoa hepsetus*)

Striped anchovy, also called silverside or glass minnow, are a major food

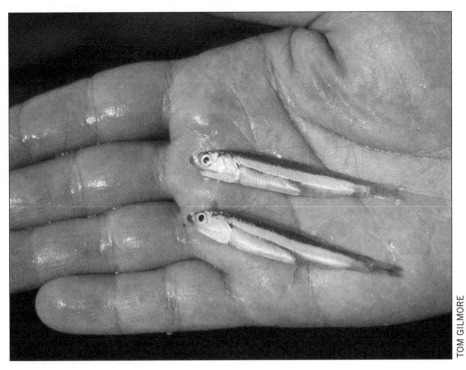

TOM GILMORE

Striped anchovy or glass minnow

source for false albacore. They range from southern New England to the Gulf of Mexico. They are particularly abundant on both coasts of Florida, making them one of the favorite baits for anglers targeting "bonito," which is what false albacore are commonly called in the Sunshine State. Striped anchovies look very similar to bay anchovies and Atlantic silversides, with a relatively large eye and a very dominant silver lateral band. They are mostly yellow-green above the band, and with the exception of their white belly, they are very translucent below this line. While they can reach 6 inches in length, they are usually in the 2- to 3-inch range.

Scaled Sardine (*Harengula jaguana* or *Herengula pensacolae*)

Scaled sardine, commonly called whitebait, greenie, or pilchard, have a southern range from northern Florida to South America. They are an important prey species for false albacore on both coasts of Florida. Because they are much hardier than striped anchovy, they are the prime choice of

Scaled sardine or pilchard and Hamilton Special fly

guides in Florida for live chum. Their bodies are wide and shaped like a boat's keel, with greenbacks and very silvery sides and belly. Their size ranges from 3 to 6 inches. Because they are fast swimmers, a quickly re-trieved fly often works best when false albacore are chasing them.

While I have described some of the major baits that false albacore target along the East Coast, this is by no means a complete list of all food sources. I have also caught albacore on squid patterns, and when there is a dearth of baitfish, I have seen albies feed on small crabs and other crus-taceans. Let's now take a closer look at the fly patterns that best imitate your region's most prevalent baitfish.

Fly Patterns and Design

Match the Hatch

Despite their speed and blitzing tactics, false albacore can be as selective as brown trout during a Trico hatch. In fly selection, there are several important elements to consider. In "hatch-matching," I find the most important element is size. Keep in mind that false albacore have relatively small mouths and little in the way of teeth. This means that they must take their prey whole, so for the most part they prefer to feed on small baits like bay anchovy, silversides, sand eels, and juvenile menhaden.

The next most important features are body shape and color. You will need to know if the body shape of the bait you are trying to match is thin like a sand eel or wide like a menhaden. As for color, I prefer my flies to match the color of the naturals on which the fish are feeding. Research suggests that false albacore have monochromatic vision and see blues and greens best. On more than one occasion, flies with some blue or green have made the difference for me. As for chartreuse, well, I just can't say enough about chartreuse. For some reason, it just works. Whether you're fishing for bonefish, bluefish, striped bass, or false albacore, don't leave home without chartreuse. As one striper fishing buddy puts it, "If it ain't chartreuse, it ain't no use!" Flash material can make the fly stand out, and it can be particularly important when you are fishing in discolored water, low-light conditions, or if there is a vast amount of bait. In clear water, I generally prefer to keep flash to a minimum.

Weight

Probably the most overlooked aspect in fly design and selection is weight and its location on the fly. Ask any guide from Cape Cod to the Florida Keys to name their top five flies, and I guarantee Bob Clouser's Deep Minnow will make the cut. Clousers are extremely effective on all species of fish. One of the main reasons they are so effective is their swimming action, which results from the location of weight on the hook. Unlike traditional methods of weighting a fly by attaching lead along the shank, the Clouser Minnow has all the weight in the front third of the hook. This allows the angler to swim, dart, or dive the fly by varying the retrieve.

Matching the prevailing bait is very important in fooling false albacore; this is especially true when the bait is concentrated. In tightly-packed schools of baitfish, your offering must look realistic enough to resemble the bait, and it must also stand out enough to be targeted. Nature's way of protecting a species is to weed out the weak or injured. Nothing triggers a predator's attack better than injured prey.

Lure manufacturers capitalize on this by manufacturing and marketing lures with names that incorporate "wounded minnow" or "crippled minnow." A fly that looks injured, fluttering or falling below or behind a tightly-packed pod of bait is almost guaranteed to be inhaled by a lurking predator. Schooling is a defense mechanism, and research proves that baitfish that look or behave differently than the rest of the school are the ones most often eaten. This effect can be achieved by varying size, shape, color, and flash, but the most effective way to have your fly stand out is to have it sink below the school. By adding weight to the front of the hook, you can make your fly dive down on a pause and dart up on a retrieve. As far as I know, Dan Blanton was the first to incorporate weight in the front of flies when he designed the Whistler Series in 1964. This style of tying proved very effective for stripers in the San Francisco Bay area. Whistlers have also been my most productive flies when fishing jungle rivers for tarpon and snook. More recently, bead or cone heads have been incorporated into patterns to achieve the same jigging motion. Today, the most popular weighted fly in the saltwater fly fisherman's arsenal is still the Clouser Minnow.

A word of caution: If a weighted fly hits your fly rod, it can crack it. To avoid this, you should open your casting loop and deliver the fly well above the rod.

Eyes

Keep in mind that you want your fly to trigger an attack by a predator fish. The action you impart on your retrieve or the flash in the fly can trigger a hit. Most of the guides I interviewed agreed that eyes are a critical component in fly design. They are the sizzle that sells the steak. Anglers often report seeing a fish "flash" behind their fly without taking it. The fish was interested but needed another clue that the offering was the real deal. If you give your fly a visible eye, I predict that your catch rate will improve dramatically. I have mentioned how effective Clousers are, and I have largely attributed their success to the jigging motion caused by the lead eyes positioned near the front of the hook. Another important characteristic of the Clouser Minnow is how prominently the eyes protrude on the side of the fly. A fish following from the rear of the fly can see the protruding Clouser eyes. In recent years, I have switched the eyes on several of my patterns from flat tape eyes to 3-D, so that they can be viewed from the rear. Eyes serve as excellent targets for predators, and that is often what they aim for. Mother Nature has even equipped several slow-swimming fish with false eyes on the rear of their bodies or even on the tails, well away from their vital organs, as a defense mechanism against predation. Several species also have eyes that are well camouflaged. Predators need trigger mechanisms—something that prods them from just following your fly to attacking it. If you want your fly to trigger a response, the eyes have it!

Traditional Patterns and Natural Materials

Traditional fly patterns like Joe Brooks' Blonde Series and Lefty Kreh's Deceivers incorporate natural materials such as bucktail and hackle into their designs. These flies are largely impressionistic and use the natural taper of the materials to shape the fly and provide movement and action. Bucktail and saddle hackle make good tail sections on flies, since they are wider and stiffer at the butt and taper toward the tips. Tying butts of hackle or bucktail to the rear of a hook gives you close to a non-fouling fly. For added foul-proofing, I add a little dab of a flexible adhesive to the butt ends after I attach them to the hook.

When chasing down high-speed, blitzing tuna, you need to be able to power a fly into the frenzy and be confident that, no matter how hard the wind is blowing or how fast your line speed, your fly won't foul around the hook. When you are finally successful at getting your fly into the strike zone, the last thing you want to worry about is a fouled fly. Fish simply won't take a fly that has fouled.

Modern Patterns and Synthetic Materials

Saltwater fly tying is really still in its infancy. Each year new materials come on the market and new patterns are developed. Traditional patterns were white, black, yellow, and combinations of blue/white or green/white, using natural materials that were dyed. Today's synthetics come in an endless array of colors and can be opaque or translucent to match local baits. Synthetics are generally more durable than natural materials, and when combined with epoxy or silicone, they make bulletproof flies.

In 1990, Bob Popovics's Surf Candy Series debuted in an article written for *American Angler & Fly Tyer* magazine by Ed Jaworowski, and the fly tying epoxy revolution was launched. Today, there is a small army of innovative East Coast tiers leading the revolution in fly design. Comprised of epoxies, silicones, and synthetics, along with traditional natural materials, today's flies are realistic, cast like bullets, and withstand the test of any predator. Albie offerings, in particular, should be very durable. If you are surrounded by pods of blitzing fish, you don't want to waste time and miss opportunities by changing flies a lot.

The Deadly Dozen

Before venturing out to interview over 50 guides for this book, I thought it would be impossible to limit the featured flies to just the "deadly dozen." However, there was remarkable consensus on a limited number of patterns. As you might expect, Clousers and Deceivers, with some regional variations, made the top of everyone's list. These were followed closely by Bob Popovics's Surf Candy, the fly that revolutionized fly fishing for false albacore. The Candy, or some local variation on the same theme, made every guide's list from Cape Cod to the Keys. Capt. Paul Dixon, who with his To the Point Charters, introduced the world to the spectacular autumn false albacore run at Montauk, had this to say: "If it were not for Bobby, we wouldn't have the false albacore fishing we do. The early days of this fishery were tough; Surf Candies and their many variations have brought albie fishing to a new level. False albacore fishermen all along the coast owe a debt of gratitude to Bob and his Surf Candy."

Another up-and-coming pattern that has caught fire in several regions is Capt. Joe Blados' Crease Fly, a surface fly that can seem to sponta-

Bob Clouser fools a false albacore with his famous Clouser Minnow

neously generate albacore out of nowhere. The other eight patterns making up the deadly dozen are all strong regional favorites.

Clouser's Deep Minnow

Bob Clouser originally designed his Deep Minnow in 1985 for smallmouth bass on his home river, the Susquehanna, in south-central Pennsylvania. While the fly is a great smallmouth pattern, it has proven deadly on almost every species of fish I have presented it to. Lefty Kreh, who designed the Deceiver, has said that if he had only one fly to fish for all the species in the world, it would be a Clouser Minnow. Lefty, true to his word, has caught over 80 species of fish on this fly. Its incredible success is due to its action in the water. Because the weighted eyes are near the front of the hook, the fly darts up on the strip and dives down on the pause. By design, it never stops moving. Even if you're not moving it, the weighted eyes are. I have lost count of the number of albacore I have taken just by letting this fly free-fall like a dead baitfish.

Tom Earnhardt, author of *Fly Fishing the Tidewaters* and the angler who introduced the fly-fishing world to the great false albacore run at Cape Lookout, North Carolina, fishes a variation of the Clouser Minnow. He calls it the Alba Clouser. Tom found his catch rate improved when he switched from traditional fly patterns to Clouser's Deep Minnow tied with bucktail, and it increased again when he tied his Clousers with synthetics. Tom uses translucent synthetics to imitate silversides and bay anchovies, which are the predominant baits in his area. He uses Ultra Hair or Super Hair in olive and polar white with silver flash for clear water, and chartreuse and polar white with gold flash for murky water or low light. For saltwater applications, I prefer to change the color of the lead eyes to a silver iris with a black pupil, which better imitates our inshore baitfish than the traditional red irises Bob tied to imitate juvenile smallmouth bass.

Clouser's Deep Minnow

Hook:	Standard-length saltwater hook sizes 2 & 1/0
Thread:	Monocord the color of the top bucktail
Wing:	Blue, green, chartreuse, gray, or olive bucktail over white bucktail and silver flash
Throat:	White bucktail
Eyes:	Lead dumbbell eyes, painted silver with black pupils, tied on the top of the hook

An albie with a Lefty's Deceiver in its mouth

Deceivers

Lefty Kreh developed his Deceiver in the late 1950s for catching stripers in the Chesapeake Bay. The Deceiver is the most widely used and copied pattern by fly fishermen on the East Coast. Lefty has taken over 100 species of fish on this fly. It's actually not a pattern, but rather a style of tying. You can imitate any baitfish from diminutive sand eels to giant bunker with a Deceiver-style fly. Professional fly tier Dave Skok ties a very sparse #2 Deceiver using two thin, white saddle hackles, with very sparse white bucktail on the bottom and sides and green or blue bucktail on top. Dave calls this fly his Bonito Deceiver, and in 1994 it earned him a 6-pound tippet class world-record 10-pound, 7-ounce bonito while fishing with Capt. Steve Burnett off Watch Hill, Rhode Island. Ken Vanderlask, a shore guide and master at taking false albacore and bonito from the beaches of Martha's Vineyard, has had tremendous success using sparse white #4 Deceivers for false albacore.

When "hard tails" are feeding on sand eels and silversides, locals at the Vineyard clean up on a small, sparse, white Deceiver sold locally as the Bonito Bandit. Ed Lepore, known on the Vineyard as "Bonito Eddie," developed the Bandit. It incorporates a tail of four thin, white saddle hackles, a body of pearl Bill's Body Braid, sparse white bucktail for the

From top to bottom: Clouser Deep Minnow tied by Bob Clouser; Jiggy tied by Bob Popovics; Deceiver tied by Lefty Kreh; and Deep Candy tied by Bob Popovics

wing and belly, and small prism stick-on eyes. This can be a killer pattern when false albacore and bonito are feeding on sand eels.

Deceiver

Hook:	Standard-length saltwater hook sizes 4–1/0
Thread:	Danville flat-waxed nylon the color of the top bucktail
Tail:	Four to eight matched white saddle hackles
Body:	Pearl Mylar braid
Collar:	White bucktail extending well beyond the hook point
Wing:	Olive, green, or blue bucktail over pearl or silver flash and white bucktail
Throat:	Red crystal flash
Topping:	Peacock herl—optional
Eyes:	Self-sticking prism eyes, silver with a black pupil
*Cover eyes and thread with a light coat of epoxy.	

Surf Candy

Bob Popovics, a man Lefty calls "the most innovative fly tier I have ever known," has spent the last three decades developing a series of flies that have redefined saltwater fly tying. The signature fly in the Pop Fleye Series is his Surf Candy, which was the first pattern to use epoxy to shape and protect the entire body of the fly. Popovics's innovative use of clear, fast-drying epoxy to shape fly bodies started the epoxy revolution. He eventually replaced the original bucktail with synthetics to create incredibly durable and realistic translucent bodies that are imitative of so many of our East Coast baitfish. The Surf Candy and the Deep Candy, which incorporate the use of weight at the front of the hook, are also styles of tying. By varying the color, the amount and length of the materials, and flash, you can produce deadly imitations of baitfish such as sand eels, silversides, and bay anchovy. Candies do not absorb water, which keeps them light and makes them easier to cast. The epoxy also prevents them from fouling and makes them virtually indestructible.

Surf Candy

Hook:	Standard or short-shank saltwater hook sizes 2 & 4
Weight:	For the Deep Candy add a silver, cone, or Jiggy head
Thread:	Fine monofilament

ED JAWOROWSKI

A false albacore with a Popovics's Jiggy in its mouth

Body:	Silver Mylar tinsel or braid
Collar:	Olive, chartreuse, blue, or green Super or Ultra Hair over silver or pearl flash, over polar or white Super or Ultra Hair
Eyes:	Self-sticking prism eyes, silver with a black pupil

*Coat the fly from just behind the eye to the bend of the hook with two coats of epoxy. Red gills can be added between coats with a Sharpie marking pen.

Jiggies

The Jiggy is one of the latest in Bob Popovics's Pop Fleyes Series. Like Clouser, Popovics designed the Jiggy fly to imitate an injured baitfish. Bob's first Jiggies used a cone head behind the eye to give the fly weight and enable the angler to imitate an injured baitfish with the retrieve. The Jiggy head is more durable than Clouser eyes, especially in Popovics's local waters. New Jersey is known as "jetty country," because its coast has more rock jetties per mile than anywhere else on the East Coast. Jetties provide great platforms for anglers to target migrating game fish, but they can take their toll on the soft lead of Clouser eyes. Popovics worked with manufacturer Stu Dickens to improve on the cone heads, and together they developed the new "Jiggy Head," which is heavier than the standard cone heads, providing a greater sinking rate. It has a slight notch in front of the head, which enables you to "snug" the head up against the eye of the hook, preventing the head from rotating. The hole through the Jiggy is also slightly larger than other conehead designs, which allows it to fit over barbed hooks. The sides are flat for stick-on eyes. By varying your retrieve, the Jiggy will dart up or flutter down like a crippled natural. By varying the length and amount of material you put on the fly, the Jiggy can be tied to imitate all coastal baitfish.

Jiggy

Hook:	Long-shank saltwater hook sizes 2 & 1/0
Weight:	Silver, cone, or Jiggy head
Thread:	Fine monofilament
Wing:	Olive, blue, tan, or chartreuse bucktail over flash over white bucktail tied in just behind the Jiggy or cone head
Eyes:	Self-sticking prism eyes, silver with a black pupil

*Cover the eyes and thread wraps with a light coat of epoxy. Super Hair can be substituted for the bucktail.

Rhody Chovy

Page Rogers, a well-known commercial fly tier from Rhode Island, developed her Beach Glass Series of epoxy patterns using a material called Opalife Bodi-Braid. Her series includes silversides, peanut bunker, juvenile herring, baby butterfish, and bay anchovy. The Rhody Chovy pattern is very popular and productive along the Rhode Island breachways, the Connecticut rips, and around Montauk Point on Long Island when there are schools of bay anchovy present. Page designed the fly to imitate three important elements she feels help induce fish to strike. First, the fly nicely imitates the little "swag" belly of the bay anchovy, which is accomplished by slipping the Opalife Bodi-Braid tubing over the hook shank and folding it back under the shank to form the body. Second, the top of the fly has a mixture of copper, gold, and root beer Krystal Flash to produce the realistic "copper/auburn" colors seen on the back of the naturals. The fly is finished off with a pair of Witchcraft stick-on prism eyes and a coat of epoxy.

Rhody Chovy

Hook:	Standard or short-shank saltwater hook sizes 2 & 4

From top to bottom: Mushmouth tied by David Skok; Crease Fly tied by Brian Dowd; Slim Jim tied by Umpqua Feather Merchants; Rhody Chovy tied by Umpqua Feather Merchants

ED JAWOROWSKI

Thread:	Clear monofilament
Tail:	Polar or white Fly Fur
Body:	Opalife Bodi-Braid
Wing:	Mixture of gold, copper, and root beer Krystal Flash
Eyes:	Self-sticking prism eye, silver with a black pupil

*Cover the entire body with a light coat of epoxy.

Slim Jim

There is nothing quite like seeing tuna take a fly on the surface of the water. Their strikes appear more aggressive. Certainly, the visual component is more thrilling for the angler. The first topwater pattern that produced false albacore for me was an effective slider-type pattern developed by Page Rogers. Page's Slim Jim is still on my deadly-dozen list.

When albies are crashing through schools of sand eels, silversides, or bay anchovy on the surface, a small thin slider can be extremely effective. A rapid retrieve skitters the fly across the surface to simulate frantically fleeing bait. They can also be fished dead-drift with an occasional twitch to imitate an injured baitfish. To demonstrate its effectiveness, in one afternoon, Page hooked 22 false albacore on a Slim Jim. That's quite a feat in and of itself, but Page was fishing from shore.

Slim Jim

Hook:	Long-shank saltwater hook sizes 2 & 1/0
Thread:	Danville's flat waxed nylon—white
Tail:	Polar white Fly Fur topped with a few strands of silver or pearl Flashabou, topped with olive Fly Fur
Body:	Cover the hook shank with white Live Body Foam (¼-inch diameter). Use a waterproof marking pen to color the belly pearl or yellow and the top olive.
Lateral line:	Wide pearl Mylar tinsel—optional
Eyes:	Self-sticking prism eyes, silver with a black pupil

*Cover the entire body with a coat of epoxy.

Crease Fly

Capt. Joe Blados developed the Crease Fly, which is one of the most effective topwater flies for inshore tuna. Over the last few years, he has had dynamite action when using it in his native waters on Long Island Sound.

The Crease Fly looks alive sitting in the water and has a very realistic swimming action when you twitch it. The first time I tried the Crease Fly was in 1998, off Jupiter, Florida. We fished it with nonstop action for four straight days. After catching several fish in a row, we alternated to test other topwater patterns, but none produced like the Crease Fly.

The fly's design is both simple and revolutionary. The basic concept is to fold, or "crease," closed-cell foam around the hook and glue the sides together. The hook is positioned low in the body of the fly and acts like a keel, enabling the fly to sit in a natural upright position in the water.

Crease Fly

Hook:	Long-shank saltwater hook size 1/0
Tail:	Bucktail and flash in colors to match your local baitfish
Body:	Foam sheeting cut to shape and folded or creased around the hook shank. Glue along the bottom to hold in place. Use various waterproof marking pens to color the body to match local baitfish.
Eyes:	Self-sticking prism eyes, silver with a black pupil

*Cover the foam body with a light finish such as Gloss Coat or thinned epoxy.

Mushmouth

The Mushmouth is a relatively new pattern developed by Dave Skok. Dave is a commercial fly tier from Massachusetts, and he and his Mushmouth have gained a lot of attention since he won false albacore fly-caught shore honors in the Martha's Vineyard Derby in 2000. He came back in 2001 to catch the largest albie in all categories and also win the overall prize for the derby. Both of Dave's winning fish were over 12 pounds; the 2000 fish was landed on the Mushmouth and the 2001 fish fell to a Surf Candy. Dave developed the Mushmouth with some help from Capt. Chris Aubat. Dave and Chris had run into several pods of bonito, skipjack, and small bluefin tuna while fishing off the coast of Rhode Island. The fish were feeding on bay anchovy, and while they did catch several fish, the flies they were using tended to foul. This experience spurred Dave to develop his foul-proof and very realistic pattern.

Dave ties the Mushmouth by folding the materials behind the eye of the hook "Thunder-Creek" style, which shapes the back and belly. Using a combination of Super Hair, Angel Hair, and Flashabou in varying amounts, lengths, and colors, Dave produces very realistic baitfish imitations. He protects the fly and prevents fouling by applying Softex glue along the body. He finishes off the fly with an epoxy eye and a coat of epoxy on the head. I can personally attest to this fly's effectiveness. In August of 2000, while fishing off Martha's Vineyard with Capt. Tim Flarity, who had introduced me to the Mushmouth, I landed my first grand slam of the year on this fly. In the fall of 2001, Dave sent me a dozen flies to photograph for this publication. Since I had been doing a lot of writing and very little tying, I took eleven of the Mushmouths down to Cape Lookout, North Carolina, in November, as back-up insurance for my fishing excursion. It's a good thing I left a single fly at home to photograph, since the others had to be retired from active duty after dozens upon dozens of false albacore tore into them. Just developed in 1999, the Mushmouth has already fooled 15 species of game fish, including tarpon, dolphin, and bluefin, skipjack, bonito, and false albacore among the tunas. This pattern is destined to become a classic.

Mushmouth

Hook:	Standard-length or short-shank saltwater hook sizes 2 & 4
Thread:	Clear monofilament, fine
Tail:	White Super Hair, silver Flashabou, tied on at mid-shank, and coated with Softex glue to past the bend to prevent fouling
Belly/Back:	White Angel Hair for the belly and olive, green, or tan Angel Hair for the back. The belly and wing are tied reverse or Thunder-Creek style.
Eyes:	Self-sticking prism eyes, silver with a black pupil

*Cover eyes and thread with a light coat of epoxy.

Bonito Bunny

In recent years, the Bonito Bunny has become the go-to fly on the Vineyard and the Rhode Island breachways. This fly was developed by Vineyard tier and guide Capt. Jamie Boyle. There aren't many guides at his young age that have such experience and wisdom on the water. This is easy to understand, because for years Jamie has been mentored by Vineyard legend, Cooper "Coop" Gilkes. Every year on my annual pilgrimage, I'd see Jamie tying all day at Coop's Tackle Shop, eyes bloodshot from battling stripers into the wee hours of the night before. Interning for

Coop, Jamie graduated from fly tier to shore guide, and now books about 125 days a year on his 22-foot Pathfinder, *The Boilermaker.* He is fast becoming one of the Vineyard's top captains. Jamie's Bonito Bunny, while simple to tie, is very durable and incredibly effective. The fly is tied entirely of rabbit; a standard rabbit strip is used for the wiggle tail and a crosscut rabbit strip is palmered to form the body. The Bonito Bunny is an excellent juvenile squid pattern, and by varying the length and width of the rabbit strips, the fly can be tied to match sand eels, silversides, peanut bunker, and juvenile butterfish. Peter Jenkins, owner of The Saltwater Edge, a fly shop in Newport, Rhode Island, reports that his clients have had tremendous success chasing false albacore and bonito with white conehead Bonito Bunnies. Often, the best presentation is simply to toss it into the melee and let it sink like a dead bait. Combining the movement of a Bonito Bunny with the action created by adding the weight of a cone head is something I'll definitely want to try next season!

Bonito Bunny

Hook:	Standard saltwater hook sizes 4 & 2
Thread:	Danville's flat-waxed nylon—white
Tail:	Strip of white rabbit over a loop of 20-pound monofilament to prevent the tail from fouling. Top this off with a few strands of pearl flash.
Body:	White crosscut rabbit
Eyes:	Self-sticking prism eyes, silver with a black pupil
*Cover eyes and thread with a light coat of epoxy.	

Hamilton Special

Capt. Scott Hamilton, who guides out of Palm Beach, Florida, has developed a very productive series of flies that he ties with translucent synthetics called the Hamilton Special. Scott feels that opaque wing materials, such as bucktail, are not as effective as translucent synthetics in the clear ocean water he fishes in the Palm Beach area. Having tried all of the synthetics on the market, Scott has settled on Sea Striker nylon jig hair for the majority of the body of the fly. The nylon hair is stiffer than most synthetics on the market and it doesn't foul. Sparkle Flash and various colors of Super Hair are added to the top of the jig hair to complete the body. He finishes the fly with very large 3-D epoxy eyes. By varying the width and length of the materials, he can imitate all of the local baitfish. This fly is relatively easy to tie and is durable enough to

From top to bottom: Hamilton Special tied by Scott Hamilton; Rhody Flat
Wing tied by the late Bill Peabody; Bonito Bunny tied by Jamie Boyle; Eric's
Sand Eel tied by Tom Gilmore.

last through most of a blitz. To date, Scott has caught 33 species of salt-water fish from his home waters on the Hamilton Special.

Hamilton Special

Hook:	Short-shank or standard saltwater hook sizes 2 & 1/0
Thread:	Pearl-rod building thread
Body:	White Sea Striker nylon jig hair forms most of the body. This is topped with Sparkle Flash and Super Hair in colors to match the local baitfish.
Eyes:	3-D epoxy eye

*Cover eyes and thread with a light coat of epoxy.

Eric's Sand Eel

Sand eels are long, thin, but not very translucent baitfish. The natural taper of bucktail provides the perfect shape to imitate sand eels. The sides of their bodies are iridescent, bright, silver-pearl, making Mylar a good body choice. Eric Peterson, a professional fly tier and top-notch albie fisherman, was the first to show me the bucktail sand eel. It's the next generation of the Joe Brooks Blonde Series. As effective as the bucktail sand eel is, Eric has developed an even more realistic and effective pattern using synthetics. Sand eels swim with a slow, wiggling motion, and materials that undulate in the water work best in imitating this motion. Eric found the material he needed in a craft store, marketed under the name Craft Fir. Now it is sold through fly shops under the name of Fly Fir. It's the same material that is used in McVay's very effective bonefish pattern, the Gottcha.

Eric's Sand Eel

Hook:	Standard or long-shank saltwater hook sizes 2 & 1/0
Thread:	Clear monofilament
Tail:	White Fly Fur or Craft Fir
Body:	Pearl Mylar braid
Wing:	Olive Fly Fur or Craft Fir tied down on top of the length of the hook shank
Eyes:	Self-sticking prism eyes, silver with a black pupil

*Cover the entire body with a light coat of epoxy.

Rhody Flat Wing

The Flat Wing is a style of tying originated and popularized by author and artist Kenny Abrames. The Rhody Flat Wing pattern was developed by the late Bill Peabody. Bill combined the Flat Wing hackle style of tying with the colors used in author and tier Ray Bondorew's Ray's Fly to develop the Rhody Flat Wing. By varying the colors and amount of materials and flash, you can imitate all of the coastal baitfish. Tied sparsely, the fly casts well and is extremely effective on all Northeast saltwater game fish. One of my fishing partners and a regular on the Rhody breachways during the fall false albacore run, Ed Janiga, has reported several epic days when fishing white or cream Rhody Flat Wings with peacock herl topping.

Rhody Flat Wing

Hook:	Standard or short-shank saltwater hook sizes 2 & 1/0
Thread:	White 3/0 monocord
Tail:	White bucktail, olive saddle hackle tied flat—curve down
Body:	Pearl Mylar braid
Collar:	White bucktail
Wing:	Sparse yellow bucktail; sparse light blue bucktail; a few strands of pearl and olive Krystal Flash; sparse olive bucktail
Topping:	Peacock herl

Hooks

Most fly fishermen spend a great deal of time and money selecting fly rods and reels and very little time and money on their terminal tackle. I believe they have their priorities reversed. I'll never forget a discussion I had with a chap who joined our group on a tarpon trip to Belize. Between his rod, reel, lodge fees, and airfare, he must have spent over three thousand dollars to pursue tarpon. However, he tied his tarpon flies on a very inexpensive brand-name hook (one that had straightened out on me on more than one occasion, costing me several big albacore and the striped bass of a lifetime). After discussing my past failure with this hook, I offered him a few of my tarpon flies, which were tied on good-quality, heavy wire hooks. These hooks had held up to tarpon, false albacore, and big bass. He admired the flies and asked how much the hooks cost. When I told him about fifty cents a piece, he was outraged. He told me he would never spend fifty cents on a hook. Two days later, after having his picture taken with a 70-pound tarpon he had taken on one of my flies, he sheepishly admitted that the fifty cents was well spent. (I didn't point out that it had been my fifty cents.)

The hook is your connection to the fish. If your hook fails, nothing else matters. A good, strong, sharp hook is literally worth its weight in gold. Many saltwater fly fishermen, like that chap in Belize, think nothing of spending thousands of dollars on vehicles and boats, and hundreds of dollars on rods and reels. They purchase neoprene waders, Gore-Tex jackets, fashionable Tarpon Wear, but wouldn't dream of spending fifty cents on a good hook. How many fish of a lifetime have been lost because your beach buggy was old or didn't have all the newest bells and whistles? Or because you were wearing worn jeans and a five-dollar T-shirt instead of Tarpon Wear? The answer is zero! I can't stress enough the importance of investing in good-quality hooks that can hold sharp points and are strong enough not to open on a good fish. Priorities in spending money on tackle should start with a good hook, a well-constructed fly, and quality tippet material, and then work back to the rod and reel. If you don't get the terminal tackle right, the rest won't change your success rate.

Delivering the Groceries: Fishing Tactics and Techniques

Reading the Water

When you are fishing an area for the first time and there are no obvious signs of feeding fish, such as nervous water, birds working, or fish busting, where do you fish? How do you determine where fish are most likely to show or where their dinner is going to be served? Let's take a look at how to locate and present your fly into likely feeding zones.

While I have taken false albacore at slack tide and in calm, flat tidal ponds and bays, they feed best when you find them in strong tidal flows. Current is the key; strong currents funnel large volumes of bait, which will hold albies' attention and keep them in the feeding zone longer. They often feed in predictable patterns, moving from one location to the next, and then repeating the cycle several times during the feeding period.

Once you have found a known feeding zone, blind casting is often productive, even when fish are not showing. One autumn morning, Capt. Joe Keegan and I were sitting in his boat off Race Rock in Long Island Sound, waiting for the tide to turn and the rip to set up. Joe suggested that I make a few blind casts, as there had been reports of albies in the area for several days. He pointed out that albies often don't show on top until the rip really starts to run hard. On my third halfhearted cast, I was fast into a speedster, and after several powerful runs Joe tailed a nice 12-pound albie. I took three albies that morning, all caught blind casting while waiting for the fish to show as the incoming tide began to run. They never did show at their predicted time, but my blind casting salvaged the day. Dave Skok, who has more success catching albies from shore than

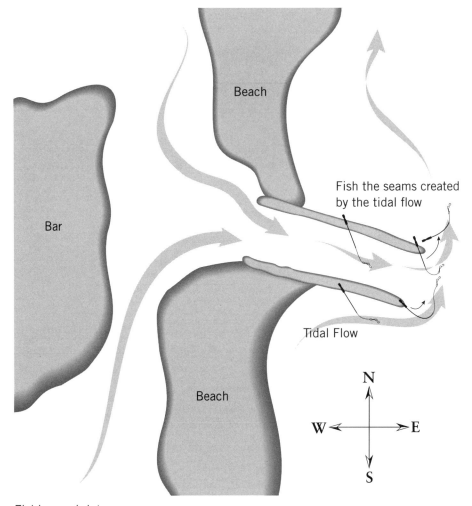

Fishing an inlet

anyone I know, reports that over 80 percent of his fish are caught while blind casting. He has had days with double-digit numbers of false albacore when there was little or no surface activity. If you are in an albie hot spot, it pays to keep your fly in the water.

As I mentioned before, the chances of intercepting these ocean speedsters will increase dramatically if you fish where structure causes the current to deliver large quantities of bait in a concentrated area.

Inlets

Inlets are narrow openings that exchange vast quantities of water between two large bodies of water and act as food funnels for predators.

Many of the better-known saltwater fishing hot spots are coastal inlets. They are productive areas because they deliver water from back bays and estuaries to the larger waters of sounds or oceans. These back bays and estuaries are literally "the cradles of the ocean," harboring young-of-the-year baitfish that spend the warmer months there to escape predation and to feed on plankton.

In the autumn, when these small fish are ready to depart on their southern migration, albies and other predators congregate at the mouths of inlets to greet them. There is no definitive right or wrong time to fish inlets, as each inlet has a different productive tide. As a general rule, when fishing from shore, I like to fish incoming tides, as predators often follow the bait as it gets pushed back inside, chasing bait pods well back into tidal ponds and estuaries. The rip line that carries bait through the inlet can swing to different sides of the inlet depending on tidal stage and wind strength and direction. It is essential to determine which side of an inlet the rip sets up on for each tide so that you can present your fly into the feeding zone.

Another important factor in choosing where to fish an inlet is the effect current from the ocean or sound has on the water coming in or out of the inlet. You'll want to be on the side that the current swings to as it leaves the protection of the inlet. This is where the bait and predators will meet. When fishing from a boat, I generally prefer a dropping tide, as the current flushes bait out of these nursery areas. Fish on dropping tides are usually feeding out of the range of shore-bound anglers.

Barden Inlet at Cape Lookout, North Carolina, Cape Poge Gut and Menemsha Inlet on Martha's Vineyard, and Quonochontaug and Weekapaug Breachways in Rhode Island are all classic albie hot spots.

Points

Points are another important structure for fishermen, as they also concentrate current and bait as the tidal waters squeeze past, often creating conditions that produce blitzes. One of the most famous points on the planet for fall blitzes is Montauk Point at the extreme eastern end of Long Island. Montauk annually produces great blitzes of striped bass, bluefish, and false albacore as the schools of bait migrating south from New England try to squeeze past the point without being detected. Mixed-species blitzes often occur close enough to shore for flyrodders to have a chance for a grand slam. Other well-known East Coast points that produce false albacore blitzes include: Great Point on Nantucket; Wasque Point on Martha's Vineyard; Napatree Point, Rhode Island; Orient and Breezy

Points, New York; Sandy Hook, New Jersey; and Cape Lookout Point on North Carolina's Outer Banks.

Reefs and Bars

Rip lines can also be caused by structures that rise up from the ocean floor, squeezing water from the bottom of the water column to the surface. This causes the water to boil or churn, disorienting the baitfish, which sets them up as easy targets for predators. One classic set of inshore reefs is located at the eastern end of Long Island Sound. The sound's waters are funneled between a series of islands and over rock structures between the islands, creating tremendous rip lines. Here, the water depth can go from 100 feet to as little as five feet in less than 100

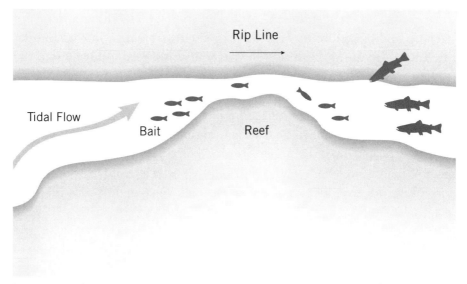

Near-shore rip

yards. Striper fishermen have long prowled such famous Long Island Sound rips as Plum Gut, the Race, and the Sluiceway. These rips are all excellent albie hot spots, as well.

Inlets, points, reefs, and bars often fish better on one tide or the other and at certain times of the tide. In my experience, the happy hour for inshore rips is often more relevant for stripers than false albacore. Tuna burn more energy and consume a higher percentage of their body weight than other inshore species and feed more frequently. I have often had a good bite for most of a tide, and then, when the tide slackened, the bait dispersed and the fishing shut off. The fishing picked up again when the next tide pushed enough water to set up a rip and again funneled the bait.

Reading the water tells us where the strike zone is most likely going to occur. Next, we have to know how to be in a position to deliver our offering. There are a few things you need to consider in order to be able to put the fly into the strike zone and keep it there.

Tactics for Shore Fishermen

Landing a false albacore from shore is one of the greatest challenges in inshore fly fishing. In terms of difficulty, I rank it right up there with stalking permit on the flats. You need to put every variable in your favor. Plan to fish the peak part of the season. Plan the tide stage you want to fish. If you can get the tide you want in low-light conditions, preferably at first light in the morning, your odds improve. Fishing at well-known shore spots during the peak of the false albacore season is rarely a solo endeavor. So plan to get into position early. If you have chosen your location wisely, it now becomes a waiting game. If you have done a good job planning and scouting and there is bait in the water in front of you, be patient but ready. Once the fish show, they can turn up in front of you with no warning, so keep your fly in the water.

I can't stress enough that position is key. Whether fishing from boat or beach, your position relative to the current that is delivering the bait is critical. Baitfish that are being sucked down-current into the mouths of predators try feverishly to swim up-current to avoid their destiny in the food chain. Your presentation location should be in a position up-current from your target area. This will allow you to cast your fly across and down and retrieve it back, swimming your fly into the current the way the naturals are facing. Predators feed on bait swimming away from them. A fly that attacks the predator rarely gets eaten and quite often will spook the fish.

When you choose your hot spot, whether it's an inlet, point, or rip, you're basically looking for moving water. When you have reduced the playing field to a smaller body of current that is funneling bait, you should be in business. Picture the current as a river and read the water as if it were a trout stream. The most successful presentation will often be the classic wet-fly swing, across and down on a tight line. This approach calls for a cast down and across the current, mending line upstream to avoid drag. Your goal is to swing the fly through the strike zone and keep it in front of the fish for as long as possible.

Many false albacore fishermen will tell you that a fast retrieve is a must. In my early pursuit of these fish, that was my approach, too, and a rapid retrieve certainly had its moments. But over the years, I have found that the true key to success is getting your offering in front of a school of false albacore and keeping it there. A slow retrieve through the strike zone presents an easier target for the fish.

Another important aspect in delivering the groceries is presenting your fly at the right depth in the water column. If I am fishing in strong current, I like to use a sinking line to get a few feet below the surface. Fish breaking on top are usually feeding well below the surface, and it's their incredible speed and momentum that carry them clear out of the water. Remember, too, that fish busting bait on top are often just the tip of the iceberg. Many more fish are feeding below the surface.

Modern sinking-head designs with floating running lines are excellent for presenting the fly deep in the water column in strong currents. The head sinks quickly and you can mend the floating running line up-current to avoid downstream drag. Drag increases the speed of the fly, pulling it out of the strike zone sooner than you want.

When fish are feeding in slower currents or slicing and churning at the surface, an intermediate or floating line works best. I particularly like the clear intermediate sinking lines that are currently on the market. Clear lines like the Scientific Anglers' Striper and Tarpon Tapers or Fly Fishing Technology's Air Flo lines work well on spooky fish in calm, clear waters. Another good alternative is Orvis' Clear Tip, which combines a 10-foot clear intermediate sink tip with a floating line. This allows for greater ease in mending line and in lifting line off the water for quick recasts.

When fish refuse your offering, there can be many reasons for their apparently selective behavior: the retrieve, a leader that is too short or too thick, a fly that is the wrong size, shape, or color, or a combination of all of these factors. Before you develop a case of albie fever and start trying an endless sequence of fly and leader combinations, understand that the fish most likely didn't refuse your fly, they just didn't see it among all the naturals, especially if there was a lot of bait in the water. If you have a good representation of the bait they're feeding on, it's probably more productive to keep your fly in the water and vary your retrieve than to constantly remove it for fly or leader changes.

I see this borne out every year on my trip to Martha's Vineyard, where hundreds of striped bass may be feeding on literally millions of sand eels. Beginning anglers that don't take fish right away usually spend the entire night changing flies to find that magic bullet. Veteran anglers fish two or three patterns of sand eels and concentrate on varying their retrieve. More often than not, all of the patterns will work on the proper retrieve. The key is getting the fish to see your offering. Even after a full night of carnage on sand eels, there are still millions of naturals merrily swimming along the beach at first light. They managed to survive by not standing out. Schooling is an effective defense mechanism, and baitfish that stand out from the school in any way are not long for this world.

The best way to make your fly stand out is to fish it on the outside edge of the schooling baitfish. Another good presentation is to fish your fly just under the school. Your fly will be seen first by albies attacking from below. Albies often crash through a school and come back and eat the dropping, injured baitfish. A weighted fly like a Clouser Minnow fished dead-drift under the bait school with an occasional twitch can be deadly. A recent addition to my albie arsenal is Joe Blados' Crease Fly. It sits upright in the water, providing a very realistic silhouette. I find a twitch-and-pause retrieve to be a killer imitation of a wounded minnow, which is irresistible to false albacore.

Tactics for Boat Fishermen

Most "sand people" think that boat fishing for albies is a sure thing. It can certainly be the easiest way to reach fish, but it is far from a sure thing. Blitzing tuna can set nerves and tempers on edge. Surface blitzes can turn mild-mannered, patient fishermen into run-and-gun addicts, resulting in what I call "boat rage." Running a boat into the middle of a school of fish not only puts them down, it splits the school into smaller pods. Thoughtless boaters can break through acres of churning albacore, leaving the area with only a handful of small pods.

There is quite a difference of opinion as to whether motors actually spook tuna. I have caught both false albacore and bonito in the prop wash, just a dozen feet behind the motor. I have also caught plenty of fish with the motor at idle. But a racing motor will almost always put them down. Some days when stemming the tide, the motor doesn't seem to bother them, on other days it quickly puts them down. On occasion, just the noise from the waves slapping against the boat has been enough to put false albacore on the run.

The best way to approach blitzing fish from a boat is to get up-current and drift down toward the fish. They will usually be feeding toward you, facing into the current. The bigger, more aggressive fish will be at the head

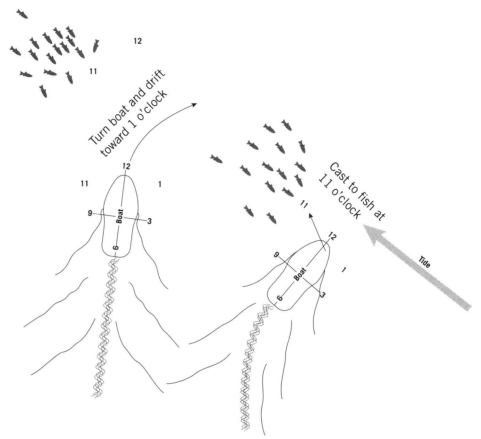

Approaching fish from a moving boat

of the school. Albies and bonito repeat attack locations, so even if fish are not showing, be patient and keep your fly in the water. I like to fish strong rips because the bait is more tightly concentrated, disoriented, and vulnerable. Albies take advantage of this and tend to feed in these rips for longer periods of time.

One of the biggest challenges when fishing from a moving boat is staying in contact with your fly. If you do motor cautiously toward a feeding school, your boat continues to drift after you cut the engine. If your cast is directly forward at the 12-o'clock position, you will most likely not be able to strip fast enough to remove slack caused by the drifting boat. If you are approaching fish at 12 o'clock, turn the boat toward 1 o'clock as you cut the motor and cast to the fish, which are now at 11 o'clock; your drift will enable you to maintain a tight line.

Casting

Fly fishing for false albacore has one big challenge not often encountered when fishing for bluefish or striped bass. That big difference is speed. False albacore often show with little warning, and the window of opportunity may be just a few seconds. This is especially true from shore, where you may only have one shot in an outing. To be successful, you need to be ready at all times. You must get the fly quickly and accurately into the fish's feeding zone and keep it there. One of the hardest things to determine is how far to "lead" the fish. There is no one right answer. It depends both on the way the bait is schooling and how the albies are feeding on the school. If the bait is dispersed, let's say along a beach front, the false albacore will most likely blitz down the beach at a good clip. During these conditions you should try to get in a position to cast your fly well ahead of the run. If you don't hook up, it pays to stay put as false albacore will often make repeat runs as long as the bait is still present. If the albies have the bait balled up tight, they will feed in an up-and-down motion, making

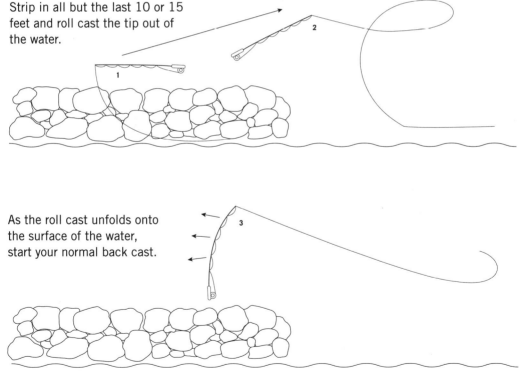

Strip in all but the last 10 or 15 feet and roll cast the tip out of the water.

As the roll cast unfolds onto the surface of the water, start your normal back cast.

Roll cast pick-up of a sinking line from a jetty

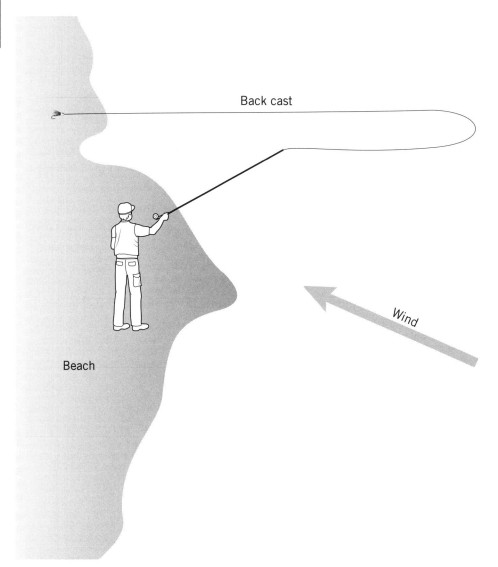

Backcasting in the wind from the beach

frequent assaults on the bait ball. Under these conditions you want your fly on the edge of the bait ball, or just below it, where it will stand out as an easy meal.

While most saltwater fish are probably caught within 50 or 60 feet of the angler, the ability to cast farther will greatly improve your chances of success. If you can cast 75 feet or more, you'll be better equipped to handle 50 to 60 feet under difficult conditions.

There are a few casting techniques that every albie chaser should

Retrieve in all but the last 10 or 15 feet of
fly line and roll cast the tip out of the water.

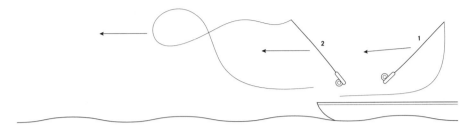

Let the roll cast unfold onto the surface of
the water. This will help load the rod on the
back cast. Between false casts you can let
your line drop on the water to reduce the
impact of wind and drift.

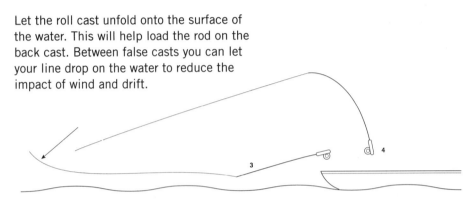

Water haul from a boat

master. First, you should be proficient at the double haul; this will enable
you to increase your line speed and load your rod with fewer false casts.
False casts waste precious time when your target is fleeing. Keeping false
casts to a minimum is crucial. You'll only have time for one or two false
casts before the fish are out of range.

Intermediate and sinking lines are harder to pick up out of the water
than floating lines due to the increased pressure of water tension. The easiest way to start a cast with these lines is to strip in all but the last 10 or
15 feet and roll-cast the tip out of the water. As the roll cast unfolds onto
the surface of the water, you can start your normal back cast (see illustration on page 93).

Dealing with wind is one of the most challenging aspects of saltwater
fly fishing. In my home state of New Jersey, the prevailing summer winds
are out of the south. Almost all of our right-handed flyrodders have developed an excellent back cast to avoid getting hit with the fly. This is
done by turning your back to the target and delivering the fly on your

back cast (see illustration on page 94). Back-casting is not just an important technique for shore-bound anglers; boat fishermen can also improve their odds by mastering this cast (see illustration on previous page). In addition to dealing with the wind, the ability to back cast will allow two boat fishermen, one in the bow and one in the stern, to cast to a school of false albacore popping up on either side of the boat.

A water haul has several advantages when chasing albacore from a boat. By using the surface tension on your line you can load your rod with less line and reduce the need to false cast. This will enable you to deliver the fly more quickly. A water haul also helps you reduce the impact of wind. By dropping the line to the water between false casts, you can greatly reduce the wind drift.

Retrieves

Generally, if the bait is spread out and the fish can find your offering among all the naturals, the best retrieve is one that closely imitates the movement of the baitfish. During these conditions, I try to imitate the natural's swimming speed and motion. On the other hand, when the bait is packed in dense bait balls, I want a fly and a retrieve that allows my offering to stand out from the pack.

Over the last few summers, I have had the opportunity to do a lot of albie chasing in Florida. The east coast of South Florida harbors huge schools of big false albacore from April through August. The prime method for finding them is to chum with live pilchards over nearshore reefs and wrecks. On my most recent trip, live chumming drew immense schools of albies that surrounded our boat for several hours each day, making for great fishing.

The presence of so many fish enabled us to experiment with different lines, leaders, tippets, flies, and retrieves to determine what worked best under these blitzing conditions. Because we were chumming, we were able to control the amount of bait. However, when we threw great quantities of bait into the water, producing heavy blitzing conditions, we found it was more difficult to hook up. Our flies just got lost in the crowd. Under these conditions, trying something radically different to make our flies stand out worked the best. Switching to a bigger fly or one with lots of flash or a bright color brought better results than exact imitations. As I mentioned before, changing the retrieve can be enough to get your offering noticed. Increasing the speed of the retrieve can trigger a response to get "the one that's getting away." A dead-drift, allowing the fly to

False albacore with a Clouser Minnow in its mouth

Fly fishing's hottest fish

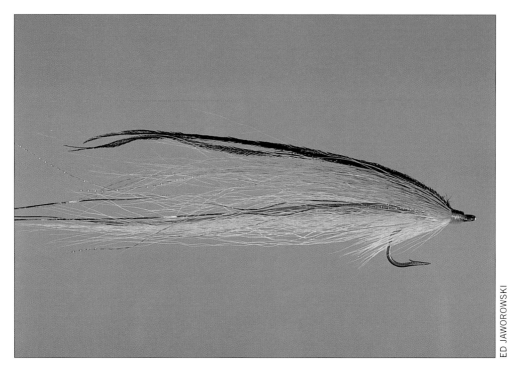

Rhody Flat Wing

Mushmouth

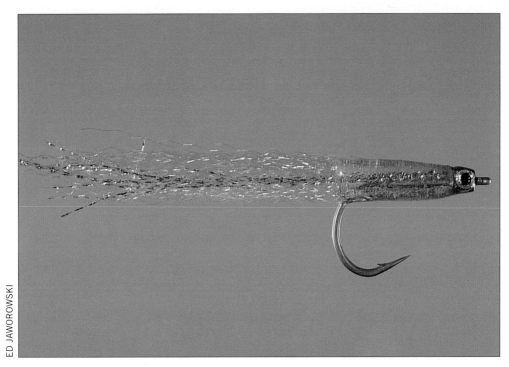

Popovics's Surf Candy

Lefty's Deceiver

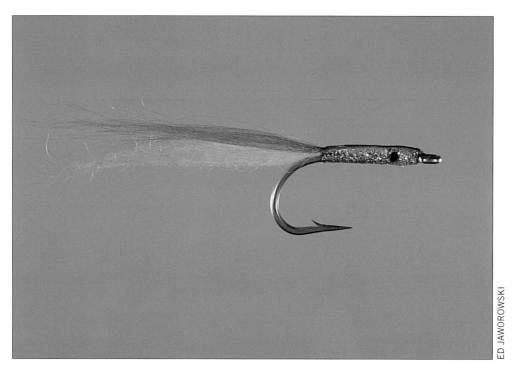

Eric's Sand Eel

Crease Fly

Hamilton Special

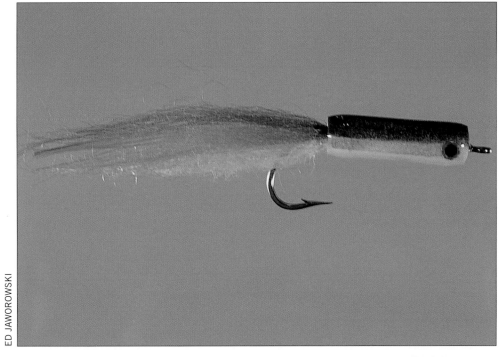

Slim Jim

Bonito Bunny

Rhody Chovy

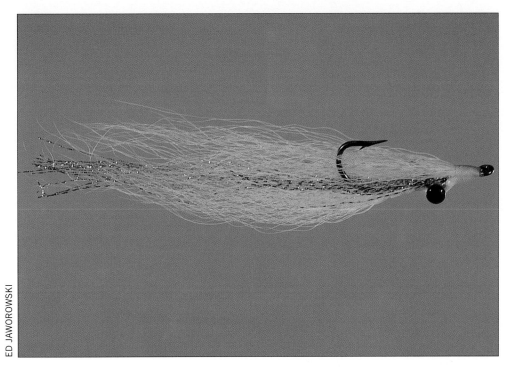

Clouser Deep Minnow

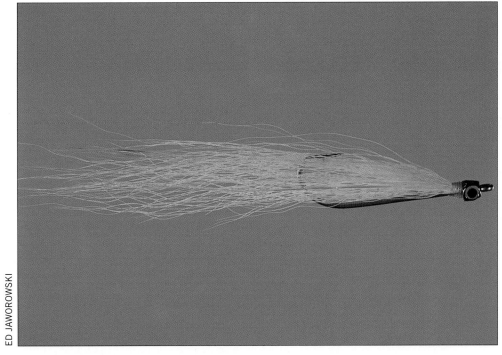

Popovics's Jiggy (Bucktail)

Two anglers hook up at Harker's Island, North Carolina

False albacore with a Popovics's Spread Fly in its mouth

flutter down with an occasional twitch to imitate an injured bait, also provides an easy target that is hard for a fish to resist. During heavy blitzes, a twitched or popped surface fly like Bob Clouser's Floating Minnow or Joe Blados' Crease Fly will draw a lot of attention.

When bait was scarce, a fly of the right size, shape, and action wouldn't last long because the fish could find our offering. If we tossed dead pilchards overboard, the fish would key into them in a few minutes, and dead-drifted flies worked much better than moving flies. Likewise, a few minutes after switching to chumming with live bait, the fish would key into the movement and a fast retrieve brought better results and more violent strikes as the albies pursued a meal that was trying to escape. Albies can get very selective and it's necessary to key into both the size and behavior of the baitfish.

I am reminded of a story I read of a young man who was totally out-fished by an old salt of an angler. The youth's casts were booming compared to his elder's, which were mediocre at best. When asked his secret, the old angler said that it's not how you put the fly out there that catches the fish, but rather how you pull it back.

One very dark night on the new moon in June, Lenny Maiorano and I were fishing over hundreds of striped bass that were sucking small sand eels from the glassy surface of Vineyard Sound. I was out-fishing Lenny by almost five to one. We tried to figure out what I was doing differently. After checking line, leader, and fly, I suggested he concentrate more on his retrieves. I told him to "be the bait," meaning to swim the fly slowly like a weak sand eel struggling against the current. Later that night, I overheard Lenny recounting the story to another member of our group. He reported that I had been hammering fish, and that while he was doing everything I was doing, he just couldn't hook up. Finally, in frustration, he said, he had resorted to what he called Gilmore's "Zen" fishing, by "being the fish." As he retrieved each cast, he kept saying, "I'm a hungry striper. I'm a hungry striper." By imitating the hungry predator, his retrieve was too fast. The next night, after realizing his mistake, he took my advice to be the prey, and with the slower retrieve, Lenny hooked into some very nice fish.

Battle Plans

Nothing you do, short of hooking the bumper of a speeding sport-utility vehicle, will prepare you for the first time you hook into a false albacore. From the second you hook up, you must be prepared for utter chaos, loose line flying through the guides and backing melting from your reel. You simply won't believe the swiftness and length of the first run. Later in the fight, you will marvel at the albie's sheer power as you try to pry it from the depths below. And it all starts with a successful hook set.

Hooking

How do you set the hook on a fish that takes your fly as fast as a false albacore does? Very carefully! How to set the hook is probably the hardest thing for newcomers to saltwater angling to learn. It is essential to turn off some of your basic instincts and learn to wait until you feel the fish strike. Prematurely striking when a fish boils or crashes on a fly will usually result in a miss—and most likely a spooked fish. In most fishing situations, whether it's fly fishing for trout, plugging the beach with a spinning rod, or deep-sea fishing over wrecks, you are taught to set the hook by lifting the rod tip.

In saltwater fly fishing, lifting the rod tip is the least effective way to set the hook. Saltwater fish have hard mouths, and the tip of your fly rod does not have the power to drive the hook home. This is especially true when you have a lot of line in the water or when fishing a sinking line. Just the weight of the line will absorb all the power a rod tip can deliver.

A more effective method is to point your rod tip straight at the fly and to strike with your stripping hand. This is called a "strip strike." Anyone who has fished with a good bonefish guide has probably noticed that they never tell you to set the hook. Instead, they say, "Strip, strip, long strip." When they mention long strip, they are actually telling you to set the hook without having you panic. If you miss a fish on a strip strike, your fly is still in the feeding zone and you often get another chance. If you miss setting the hook by lifting your rod high, the fly most likely will be moved well out of the fish's range.

If you prefer to use a two-handed retrieve with the rod tucked under your arm, the tendency is not to lift the rod but to set the hook with whichever hand is moving the fly when the fish hits. You don't need to strike hard, especially if the fish is going away when it hits. It is important that the strike be short in both time and distance. One quick, short set is enough for the hook to penetrate and will minimize the chance of breaking the tippet. Quite often, false albacore hook themselves by swimming up behind the fly, taking it, and turning away. In many cases, their sheer speed tightens the line before the angler knows the fish has taken the fly.

When false albacore are blitzing on top, porpoising, or rocketing out of the water and causing frantic baitfish to skip or jump for their lives, they often will attack your fly the second it hits the water. In order to be prepared to strike right away, you need to have your fly line under control during your cast. The best way to do this is to form a circle around the line with the thumb and index finger of your line hand as you shoot the cast. This can act as an additional stripping guide. As the fly approaches the target, just close your hand and you are ready to strip in line. This method also prevents the line from wrapping around your reel or the rod butt. While you should always be ready to set the hook or retrieve when your fly hits the water, often you'll need to let the fly sink to the feeding level of the fish. At all times, keep your rod pointed at, and be in contact with, your fly. As soon as the fish is hooked, ease up on the pressure and concentrate on clearing line to the reel.

Clearing Line to the Reel

Hooking a false albacore is actually the easy part. Getting the loose line on the reel is the most difficult part of the battle and the time when most fish are lost. Unless the fish hits the moment the fly touches the water, you will have loose line in your stripping basket or on the boat deck as a result of stripping the fly in during the retrieve. This line will literally fly through the guides in a heartbeat. Remember, at 40 mph, an albacore can cover the length of a football field in 7 seconds. Your eyes should concentrate on the excess line, not the fish, until all the loose line has cleared the rod's guides and your reel starts to sing. Doing this correctly will dramatically increase the odds of landing the fish. Here are some tips to help you successfully clear your line and get the fish on the reel:

- As soon as a hooked fish starts its blistering first run, you need to get your line under control and "clear" it to the reel. With your stripping hand, hold the line out and away from your rod butt and reel, applying light pressure on the line as the fish pulls it out. *Do not*, I repeat, *do not* form a loose circle with your thumb and index finger. Instead, put some light pressure on the line so that it will not jump out of control and wrap around the reel, rod butt, or other obstacles. I like to hold the rod high and away from my line hand, with the butt pressing against my wrist so that the line can't wrap around it. Once your loose line is on the reel, your drag will start to earn the money you spent on it.

- Dress for success. Yes, your choice of clothing can literally make or break your first date with Mr. Speed. Anything that can catch your fly line will catch your fly line and cause a break off. This is especially true of shoestrings, raingear, hip pliers, stripping baskets, and jewelry. Starting from head to toe, the most likely line-grabber is the shirt cuff on the wrist of your stripping hand. A large button on the cuff of your shirt, or the Velcro cuffs that are so popular on raingear, can be problematic. If weather permits, wear a short-sleeved shirt or roll up the sleeve on your stripping hand. Just last summer, I lost a double-digit fish to a button on my Tarpon Wear shirt that sits above the elbow to hold a rolled-up sleeve. Avoid wearing a watch or neck jewelry, as they have a knack for grabbing loose line. Wearing a neck lanyard for holding clippers or other tools is really asking for trouble. If you wear pliers on your belt, keep them on the hip of your casting arm, not on your stripping side, where your loose line may fall and catch during the battle.

- Footwear also requires special consideration. For safety reasons, if you're fishing from a jetty, corkers or cleats are a must. If your shoes have laces, make certain that they are tucked or, better yet, taped safely away. When fishing from a boat in warm weather, I like to fish barefoot so that I can feel when I am stepping on the line. Lefty Kreh has a great tip for wearing boat shoes; he ties his laces in a square knot and cuts away the tag ends. Then he just slips them on and off like a pair of loafers.

- When fishing from the beach, make certain that your stripping basket, raingear, chest pack, or vest don't have loose ends or tools hanging off that can grab a line.
- Most fly-fishing guides have usually done a good job of removing obstacles from their boats. It's still a good idea to bring a towel or two that can be draped over obstacles that could catch fly lines. Wet the towels so they will stay in place.

The Fight

Once you have the fish "on the reel," you can concentrate on fighting it. If you are wearing a stripping basket, now is the time to move it out of your way and around to your back. This will allow you to see where you're stepping and freely fight the fish. As mentioned earlier, a good rule of thumb in fighting all saltwater game fish is that your line should always be moving: Either the fish is gaining line or the angler is.

Bob Popovics fighting a false albacore in the rip off the North Jetty at Barnegat Inlet, New Jersey.

During the early stages of the battle, the fish will be in control, peeling off as much as 100 yards of line or more on the initial run. Don't apply too much pressure on the first run. I set my drag fairly light, at about 4 pounds of pressure. If necessary, I can apply additional pressure on the exposed rim of the reel with the palm of my free hand. When the fish tires on the first run, it will often turn back and tear off in a different direction. This action usually causes your line to go slack. If this happens, reel as fast as possible, even if you think you have lost the fish. Nine times out of ten, you just need to get the slack out of the line and the battle will resume. It's a good idea to drop your rod tip into the water as you reel in the slack line. This will prevent the slack line from wrapping around the rod tip and snapping off your fish.

I will never forget a story relayed to me by a newcomer to flyfishing about landing his first bonito. He had fished over breaking fish for more than two hours with no results. Then, on one cast, he hooked three bonito, losing the first two before he landed the third fish of the cast. After releasing the fish, he couldn't buy a hit for the rest of the day, even though there were plenty of bonito feeding. He asked me how one cast could have been so productive. I concluded that he had hooked only one fish, and that each time it changed direction, his line would go slack, giving the feeling of a lost fish. As he continued to reel, he was taking the slack out of the line. Eventually, when the line would again become tight, it felt like he had hooked another fish, but he had really just caught up with the same fish again.

After the first few runs, the fish will really begin to tire and you must take control of the battle and begin to gain line. The most efficient way to do this is to press the rod's fighting butt against your stomach for leverage and "pump" the rod, pulling the fish toward you and then lowering the rod back toward the fish while reeling in the line. The strongest part of a rod is the butt, yet so many anglers like to hold the rod high and fight the fish with the tip of the rod. This puts a good-looking bend in the rod but very little pressure on the fish. Keeping the angle of the rod low lets you fight the fish with the power of the butt section. Once the angle of the rod exceeds 45 degrees, the pressure on the rod tip increases and the pressure on the fish diminishes. The higher you go toward 90 degrees, the more stress and pressure you have on the rod tip and the more likely you are to break the rod. False albacore have the heart of a lion, and they will fight you until they are totally exhausted. The shorter you make the fight, the greater chance the fish has of surviving. That is why I recommend at least a 10-weight rod to give you the lifting power to land a tuna in short order.

Fighting Fish from Shore

When fishing from a gently sloping, sandy beach, you often get very long runs out of fish because the relatively shallow water forces the fish to go out, as there is no "down." In most cases, the fish will run down-current along the beach. If you are wading, it's a good idea to get out of the water and follow the fish. Remember, the more line between you and the fish, the less control you have, so stay as close to your catch as you can. Keep the rod low to the side, again exerting pressure with the butt of the rod. As the fish comes into the shallows, the best way to land it is to slide it up onto the beach.

If you're fishing big surf, you must take care to work with the waves, not against them. With the rod low to the side, keep pressure on the fish. Time your landing of the fish with the force of the wave. On the first try in big surf, the fish can be sucked back down the beach in the backwash. Don't try to fight the movement of the fish and the wave; keep slight pressure on the fish and follow it back down the beach and wait for the next wave to help you beach it.

Fishing for false albacore from a rock jetty can be very productive if you plan carefully. Before you start fishing, determine a safe spot where you can land a fish. If you are fishing inside an inlet from a jetty, determine if there is a relatively safe rock to climb down to land a fish. When fishing the outside edge of a jetty, the best option, if available, is to walk back to shore and beach the fish. If you plan to do this, start heading back when the fish is still reasonably far out, so that you can avoid having to fight it around the rocks as you near the shore.

Fighting Fish from a Boat

You will not be able to turn a tuna and bring it directly to the boat; instead, the fight will become circular around the boat. Eventually, the circles will come tight to the boat and the fish will start to cross in front of the bow or behind the stern. Resist trying to keep the fish on your side of the boat. Go with it, walking to the bow or stern and extending the rod so the line clears the boat. This is especially important at the stern, as you need to clear the engine and propeller. I have had albies circle the boat as many as three times before they could be landed. Doing the albie shuffle can get chaotic when you have two anglers circling at the same time, especially, when they're going in different directions. If the lines start to

ED JAWOROWSKI

Bob Clouser lands a false albacore at Harkers Island, North Carolina

cross, go toward the fish; don't try to pull back or the lines will wrap multiple times. If the lines have crisscrossed, the best way to remedy the situation is to bring the rod tips together. This will show you which line is over and which is under, enabling you to straighten out the lines and land both fish. I have seen a party boat with a rail full of novice anglers, all hooked into false albacore, going in every direction. This caused lines to tangle into such a spider web that the mate had no choice but to walk the rail and cut the lines rather than deal with the mess.

Eventually, as the fish gets closer (within 15 to 20 feet), the circles get tighter and you will have to lift the fish's head up to unscrew it from the depths below. Lift the fish toward the direction it is circling—lifting up and reeling down. A slow, steady lift works best. Pump the rod by raising it from a horizontal position toward a vertical position, but again, never go beyond 45 degrees. Be ready to give ground if the fish bolts. Do this by lowering the rod tip and extending your arms toward the fish.

Next comes "crunch time," when the fish is just about to be landed. This is the time when many anglers watch the fish and give that last little pull with the rod tip pointed straight up. This is known as high-sticking, and it is often the cause of rods being broken. The best way to move the fish those last few feet to your partner or guide for landing is to keep the rod low and just take a step or two back, pulling the fish to the boat. Once the fish is at the water's surface, the easiest way to land it is to have your partner grab it at the narrow portion located in front of the tail.

The Release

False albacore have negative buoyancy; if they are motionless, they sink. Albies never rest and must continuously swim forward. It's literally a sink-or-swim proposition. The traditional method of reviving a fish by holding it upright and moving it back and forth in the water will kill a false albacore. Tuna are built to constantly move forward. They don't cycle water past their gills when they are motionless. The best release is to toss or lob them into the water headfirst at a 45-degree angle. This sends a surge of oxygen over the gills and usually jump-starts them.

Related Species

All 13 of the world's tuna species belong to the Scombridae family of mackerels. Tuna are found in most of the world and have long been valued as a food fish. Canned tuna is convenient, relatively inexpensive, and outsells all other types of canned meats worldwide. Americans alone consume more than 400,000 metric tons of canned tuna a year. Due to over-harvesting worldwide, tuna stocks have been declining for the last three decades. In the Atlantic Ocean, they have declined roughly 90 percent.

One of the great challenges facing fisheries management in the new millennium will be regulating tuna harvest to support sustainable levels of reproduction. Five of the eight Atlantic tuna species are regulated, with over 20,000 permitted vessels participating in tuna fisheries management programs. Only blackfin, bonito, and false albacore remain unregulated and, therefore, unprotected. Tuna are a schooling fish, and they feed on other schooling fish. Because tuna require vast amounts of food, they are highly migratory, with their movements closely linked to the fishes on which they feed and to water temperature. They are found worldwide in tropical and temperate seas only, as they cannot tolerant temperatures below 50 to 54 degrees Fahrenheit.

Flyrodding for tuna has gained tremendous popularity since the fall of 1991, when Steve Able chartered a 113-foot boat, the *Royal Polaris* out of San Diego, for the first-ever big-game bluewater fly fishing trip. This opened a new era in fly fishing, and numerous world records were broken, especially for yellowfin and skipjack tuna. Flyrodding for any member of the tuna family is a tremendous sport. Pound for pound, the tunas fight with more strength and endurance than any other fish in the world. Here is a brief synopsis of the status of fly fishing for the most popular Atlantic coast species of tuna.

Atlantic Bonito (*Sarda sarda*)

Description

Atlantic bonito are one of the most beautiful fish that swim our oceans. In fact, in Spanish "bonito" means beautiful. They are smaller than their inshore cousin, false albacore. Bonito average 5 to 7 pounds, with a 9- or 10-pound fish being a real trophy. Bonito can be distinguished from false albacore by the series of seven or more dark, wavy horizontal lines on the upper half of their backs, compared to the dark, jagged, mackerel-like markings on the upper backs of false albacore. Bonitos' backs are blue-green and their bellies are silver to whitish. They have very short pectoral fins, and there are 20 to 23 fin rays on the first dorsal, 13 to 18 fin rays on their second dorsal, followed by 7 to 10 finlets. Additionally, their dorsal fins are long, low, and not divided. By comparison, false albacore have a higher dorsal fin, and the base only runs a short distance on their backs. Bonito lack the definitive belly spots or fingerprints of false albacore. They can be easily distinguished from skipjack, which have stripes on their belly instead of the back. Unlike false albacore, bonito make great table fare.

Distribution

Bonito are found in the tropical and temperate waters of the Atlantic Ocean from Nova Scotia to Argentina. They are rare migrants into the Gulf of Mexico. They spend most of their time feeding 15 to 20 miles offshore, but bonito, like false albacore, are unusual in the tuna world because they often come inshore and even into inlets, bays, and estuaries, giving the wading fisherman an opportunity to land an offshore species from shore. Bonito are more tolerant of cool water than false albacore, so they arrive inshore earlier and stay longer. In the Northeast, Bonito arrive earliest in the waters around Nantucket and Martha's Vineyard in late July, when the water warms into the mid-60s. They come in from the Gulf Stream on plumes that break off from the main current. In the Northeast the best fishing for bonito is from late July until around Labor Day, which is when the false albacore start arriving in numbers. As the

The author with a bonito off Stonington, Connecticut

numbers of false albacore build, they tend to push out the bonito. A second run of bonito occurs in the Northeast in late October and, in some years, early November, after the false albacore leave when the waters begin to drop into the mid-50s. Bonito are not nearly as common as false albacore in the waters off the Outer Banks of North Carolina, but there is a fishable spring run.

Fly Fishing

Most fly fishermen agree that bonito seem to have better eyesight than false albacore, and they can be more selective. Keen eyesight makes them leader-shy, and most bonito fishermen use light tippets of 8- to 12-pound test. Also, the use of fluorocarbon has become very popular in the last few years. Bonito have small mouths with large, pointy, conical teeth. Fortunately, their teeth are spaced and they don't go all the way to the corner of the jaw. Since most fish are hooked in the corner of the mouth, you usually don't need a shock tippet. After a hook-up, it's a good practice to check your tippet for nicks. Flies should generally be small, sparse, and match the local baitfish. Bonito have tough mouths, so sharp hooks are a necessity. Because these fish grab bait with their teeth, they tend to short-strike or nip the back of the bait or fly. Flies should have very short tails, and I have learned that a long-shanked hook will outperform a standard hook. Most bonito anglers use 8- or 9-weight rods. Reels should have smooth drags and hold 150 yards of 30-pound backing.

Hot Spots

In the Atlantic Ocean, there are two viable areas to target inshore bonito with a fly rod. The coastal waters of the Northeast provide the best opportunity for large bonito, with all 13 of the fly rod tippet class world records (1 is vacant) and 4 line class world records coming from an area local anglers call the Bonito Triangle. The triangle runs from the eastern end of Long Island northeast to Martha's Vineyard and west to the Rhode Island Breachways. Bonito arrive in these waters in late July and often stay until the first week of November. They are attracted to this area by the numerous salt ponds and estuaries, which harbor incredible quantities of baitfish. These waters are the first to warm along the Northeast coast. The outflows and inlets that connect the ponds to the ocean offer the shore-bound angler legitimate shots at inshore tuna.

Every spring, the southern coast of North Carolina gets a push of bonito from Morehead City and Atlantic Beach south to the waters around Cape Fear, Wrightsville Beach, and just outside Masonboro Inlet.

The fish arrive in early April and peak in mid-April to early May before heading offshore to the waters of the Gulf Stream. While these bonito are relatively small, averaging around 3 to 6 pounds, they form massive schools on nearshore reefs and wrecks. You can usually spot them from a distance by the circling birds and churning white water as they crash through schools of bay anchovies and silversides.

Records

D. Gama Higgs holds the IGFA all-tackle record for Atlantic bonito at 18 pounds, 4 ounces. He caught it on July 8, 1953, near Faial Island in the Canary Islands off the coast of Spain. As I mentioned earlier, all of the fly rod tippet class, and several of the line class world records come from an area that has been dubbed the Bonito Triangle, and all are fairly recent catches. These record fish were taken from early August to early November, with most of the bigger fish being taken from late October into the first few days of November. You will note that no records were recorded in September, which is usually when the more aggressive false albacore arrive in the greatest numbers in the Bonito Triangle and push bonito out of the area. That's not to say that I haven't had days when I did well on both species, but usually when I take both species in the same day, it's from different feeding areas.

Current IGFA Fly Rod Records for Bonito

Tippet	Weight (lbs./oz.)	Location	Angler	Date
Male				
2	5/15	Montauk, NY	S. Sloan	8/12/88
4	8/6	Weekapaug, RI	J. Dickinson	11/2/90
6	10/7	Fishers Island, NY	D. Skok	10/27/94
8	10/9	Martha's Vineyard, MA	K. Bramhall	10/3/89
12	12/5	Martha's Vineyard, MA	J. Lepage	10/23/94
16	7/4	Mt. Sinai Inlet, NY	C. Catan	11/3/95
20	8/4	Groton, CT	J. Balint	10/5/97
Female				
2	Vacant			
4	5/0	Watch Hill, RI	Gail Noyes	8/14/00
6	5/8	Watch Hill, RI	Gail Noyes	8/15/98
8	5/8	Quonochontaug, RI	Gail Noyes	8/17/98
12	8/2	Watch Hill, RI	Gail Noyes	10/31/99

| 16 | 7/0 | Weekapaug, RI | Gail Noyes | 8/14/98 |
| 20 | 5/8 | Watch Hill, RI | Gail Noyes | 8/14/98 |

In addition to holding all six of the women's tippet class records, on October 16, 1996, Gail Greenwood Noyes landed the 16-pound line class world-record bonito. The 11-pound, 12-ounce fish is the largest bonito ever landed in the United States by a woman. All seven of Gail's records were landed while fishing with her husband and guide Captain Sandy Noyes.

Skipjack Tuna (*Katsuwonus pelamis*)

Description

Skipjack tuna, also known as striped tuna and oceanic bonito, are more tapered at both ends than false albacore, giving them more of a cigar-shaped body with a sharply pointed snout. They are dark blue on top

Dave Skok with a skipjack

with silvery sides and bellies. The presence of four to six horizontal stripes on the belly and the absence of markings on the back distinguish skipjack tuna from other tuna species. Their mouths are relatively large, and like bonito, they have small, conical teeth. While they can exceed 40 pounds, skipjack tend to average only 5 to 10 pounds, with fish in the teens being real trophies.

Distribution

Skipjack tuna have worldwide distribution in tropical and temperate seas and can be found in the Atlantic as far north as Massachusetts in the summer and as far south as Brazil year-round. They are common throughout the Gulf of Mexico. Skipjack can form vast schools when feeding near the surface, with numbers as high as 50,000 fish. They often join in with blackfin and yellowfin tuna during a feeding frenzy.

Fly Fishing

Pound for pound, many guides feel that skipjack are the toughest tuna to tangle with on a fly rod. They are primarily an offshore fish, making only rare inshore appearances. Offshore boat captains have nicknamed them "mushmouths," due to their relatively soft mouths. Great care should be used when applying pressure to these fish, especially during the early stages of the battle. Rods of 8- to 10-weight and reels with smooth drags and capacity for 200 yards of 30-pound backing will match nicely for skipjack.

Records

The IGFA all-tackle record for skipjack is 45 pounds, 4 ounces. Brian Evans caught this fish off Mexico's Baja on November 16, 1996. The fly-rod record is 16 pounds, 1 ounce, taken by Walt Jennings off the Revillagigedo Islands of Mexico on March 20, 1996.

Blackfin Tuna (*Thunnus atlanticus*)

Description

Blackfin tuna, also called Bermuda tuna and blackfinned albacore, have bluish black backs, with a bronze lateral band on their upper sides. They can be easily confused with yellowfin tuna, which have a golden stripe on their backs. Blackfin have silver sides and milky-white bellies. Except for having black fins, they are very similar to yellowfin and bigeye tuna. In the Atlantic Ocean, they can range in size from a few pounds to over 30 pounds.

Distribution

Blackfin occur in tropical and warm temperate waters, with their optimum water temperature around 74 degrees Fahrenheit. They are found in the waters of the western Atlantic Ocean as far north as Martha's Vineyard, but usually their range is from North Carolina to Brazil, throughout the Caribbean, and in the Gulf of Mexico.

Fly Fishing

Blackfin can be caught year-round in tropical waters and have become a very popular fly-rod fish in the Florida Keys and the Gulf of Mexico. Spring action for blackfin tuna can be hot in southeast Florida, especially around shrimp boats as they cull their catch, creating a chum slick that re- sults in a feeding frenzy. The challenge is trying to get your fly through the thousands of false albacore that are also enjoying this free meal, but this is a challenge every coastal flyrodder should experience. A 10-weight rod is fine for fish up to 15 pounds; however, you'll often encounter fish in the 15- to 25-pound range, in which case an 11- or 12-weight rod would be a better choice. Blackfin don't have large teeth, but they can cut mono, so a shock tippet is highly recommended.

Hot Spots

Florida holds 8 fly rod tippet class records (4 are vacant) and is clearly the "hot spot" for blackfin. In addition to spring blackfin action around the shrimp boats in southeast Florida, they are also a popular fly-rod fish in the Miami area from Triumph Reef to Government Cut. The "hump" off Islamorada can also be a very hot spot. By far, the best blackfin tuna fishing is found in the Gulf of Mexico, peaking during the spring and summer, although they are available year-round. If the fish are not visible, most captains anchor up-current from seamounts or offshore wrecks or anywhere that structure causes an upwelling of water. They then chum to bring the fish within casting range.

Records

The IGFA all-tackle blackfin tuna record is 45 pounds, 8 ounces. Sam Burnett took this trophy in the waters off Key West, Florida, on May 4, 1996. The fly-rod record is 34 pounds, 3 ounces, and this fish was taken by Rip Cunningham off Islamorada, Florida, on December 17, 1977.

Atlantic Bluefin Tuna (*Thunnus thynnus*)

Atlantic bluefin, also known as northern bluefin and giant bluefin, are the largest member of the mackerel family. Bluefin tuna are the most valuable wild animal on the face of the earth. Prized as sushi, raw bluefin meat can sell for up to $50 a pound. A single fish can be worth as much as $50,000 on the Tokyo market, and one fish sold for an incredible $83,000. Unfortunately, their value has caused over-harvesting to such a point that their population has declined over 80 percent in the last 20 years.

Description

Bluefin tuna are among the largest and most wide-ranging animals on earth. They can grow to over 10 feet and 1,500 pounds. What other fish in the 100-pound range would you refer to as a schoolie? Their upper bodies are blue-black, and they have a silvery-white underbody. Their bodies are deep, rounded, and torpedo-shaped. In addition to their large size, they can also be distinguished from other tuna by their relatively short pectoral fins, which never reach as far back as their second dorsal fin.

Distribution

Bluefin tuna are found in temperate and subtropical waters all over the globe. They have a transoceanic migration pattern that can take them as far north as Norway and as far south as Brazil, making conservation of this species extremely difficult. Recently, one bluefin that was tagged in the Bahamas was caught 15 days later in Norway, some 6,200 miles away. They are very rare in the Gulf of Mexico. Bluefin can maintain a higher body temperature than any other tuna, as high as 35 degrees above the surrounding water. This capability enables them to move into the cold Canadian waters in search of prey. In colder water, they must consume as much as 25 percent of their weight each day to maintain a body temperature high enough to survive. They will feed in water temperatures in the range of 50 to 82 degrees Fahrenheit, with the optimum temperature around 68 degrees. Bluefin are primarily an offshore fish, but they do come farther inshore than albacore and bigeye tuna.

Fly Fishing

Bluefin tuna are extremely difficult to catch on a fly rod. Just finding one small enough to land can be problematic. Because of their great size, strength, and speed (up to 50 mph), tackle must be top-notch. Rods of at least 12- to 14-weight with plenty of lifting power are required to power these fish back to the boat. Large-capacity reels with strong drags are also a must. Fly lines should be short, 50 feet or less, or shooting heads like the Teeny 650 or 750, with most of the rear running line cut off to increase the reel's backing capacity. You'll need to have 400 to 500 yards of backing if you're going to stop a bluefin. Many guides prefer 50-pound Spectra for backing, as it cuts through the water better than Dacron. Flies should be large, with tandem hooks of 5/0 to 8/0, and 20-pound tippets with 100-pound shock tippet. These fish are extremely tough. If you do decide to pursue them, be prepared for crushed tackle and bruised egos. While these fish can be caught when free-feeding, most charter captains anchor and chum or chunk to bring the fish to the surface. An experienced captain can usually bring these fish to within 30 or 40 feet of the boat.

Hot Spots

Some years, bluefin show inside Block Island and lower Narragansett Bay in late July and stay into October. Captain Greg Weatherby from the Saltwater Edge Fly Shop has successfully landed small bluefin up to 25 pounds on 10-weight rods and fish up to 40 pounds on 12-weights. September and early October are prime time for giant bluefin in New England. In New York, the Butterfish Hole, which lies about 15 miles south-southwest of Montauk Point, is a renowned tuna hot spot, especially in the fall. In New Jersey, bluefin show up at the Mud Hole around the middle of June, and they are available through November. During these months, they are also found well offshore in both the Hudson and Wilmington Canyons.

The major hot spot for fly-rod bluefin tuna is off North Carolina's Outer Banks. The Outer Banks swing so far out into the Atlantic Ocean that they are the junction for the cold Labrador Current sweeping down from the north and the warm Gulf Stream flowing up from the south. Bluefin feed on the supply of food these two ocean-rivers gather as the currents meet. Large concentrations of "mediums" and "giants" gather in winter off Cape Hatteras, giving offshore anglers the best opportunity to land one of these monsters on a fly. Bluefin start showing up in late autumn and can stay into April, but January through March is prime time. Bluefin action can be as close as 1 to 5 miles off the beach. The hub of activity is out of Hatteras Harbor Marina, where conventional-gear charters can take up to two-dozen fish a day in the 120- to 175-pound range.

Capt. Steve "Creature" Coulter pioneered bluefin fly fishing in this region. In 1996, the first Hatteras bluefin was landed on a fly by Coulter, with Capt. Brian Horsley serving as his mate. From 1996 to 2000, the five largest fly-caught bluefin tuna came from Coulter's boat. Two of these were world records. Their strategy is to look for a school of bluefin that has fish small enough to tackle, and chunk-feed them until they surface. Try to imagine how exciting it would be to see a school of 100-pound-plus tuna boiling on the surface and eating chunks—and flies—within 40 feet of the boat.

Fly fishing for bluefin is still in its infancy, with four of the five fly rod class tippet records being recorded after 1995. In the fall of 2000, while working on a draft of this chapter, I noted that new innovations in tackle and technique would raise the world-record bar on all species of tuna. In hindsight, I realize that this was quite an understatement.

On Friday, January 12, 2001, angler Brad Kistler took fly fishing for tuna to a whole new level. Fishing a wreck off the Cape Lookout shoals aboard Captain Bill Harris' boat, *Fly Caster*, Kistler landed a 196-pound bluefin that has recently been accepted as the new world record, besting the previous world record by an astonishing 67 pounds. He landed this great fish in only one hour and fifteen minutes, using a Sage RPLX, 8-foot, 9-inch, 14-weight rod, Charlton 8550 reel, and 20-pound class tippet. Now that's what I call putting the pedal to the metal!

Records

Ken Frazer took the IGFA all-tackle record of 1,496 pounds off Nova Scotia, Canada, on October 26, 1979. To date, there are only five tippet class records for bluefin tuna. The rest are vacant.

Current IGFA Fly Rod Records for Bluefin

Tippet	Weight (lbs./oz.)	Location	Angler	Date
6	14/0	Montauk, NY	Steven Sloan	8/30/81
8	28/8	Indian River, DE	Rich Winnor	8/7/97
12	42/8	Virginia Beach, VA	David M. Limroth	7/20/97
16	101/8	Hatteras, NC	Raz Reid	2/22/96
20	196/9	Morehead City, NC	Bradly Kistler	1/12/01

I would be remiss if I failed to recognize Michael Reid, who landed a 128-pound Hatteras bluefin on January 23, 1996. This catch was the first fly-rod tuna over 100 pounds and stood as the world record until Stephen

Hutchins broke it on February 24, 2000, with his then-record 129-pound bluefin, also landed off Hatteras.

Yellowfin Tuna (*Thunnus albacares*)

Description

Yellowfin tuna, also known as Allison tuna, is the fish that started the long-range offshore fly fishing craze in the fall of 1991 out of San Diego, California. Yellowfin tuna have beautiful dark blue backs with a conspicuous golden-yellow lateral band on their upper sides. Their lower sides and bellies are a silver-gray color. Yellowfin are more slender than bluefin and bigeye tuna, with smaller heads and eyes. Their pectoral fin always reaches the second dorsal fin, but never beyond. Yellowfin range in size from just a few pounds to over 300 pounds. They are one of the canning industry's prime species, accounting for as much as 35 percent of the world's tuna catch, sold on the market as "chunk light" tuna.

Distribution

Yellowfin tuna are the most tropical species of tuna, preferring water temperatures from 64 to 86 degrees Fahrenheit, with 72 degrees the optimum. On the East Coast, they are found from New Jersey to the Florida Keys and throughout the Gulf of Mexico. Young fish are known to form large schools near the surface of the water, making them accessible to fly-rod anglers.

Fly Fishing

Mark Sosin landed the first recorded yellowfin tuna on a fly in July of 1969. His record wasn't broken until 1973, when Jim Lopez landed an 81-pound fish off Bermuda. Bermuda boasts some of the world's finest yellowfin tuna fishing, providing opportunities for records, including Lopez's 12- and 16-pound class tippet records. Like bluefin, yellowfin weighing over 100 pounds are very difficult to land on a fly, but increased numbers of flyrodders are targeting them. You can expect to see an assault on all of the class tippet records in the next few years. While they are an offshore, bluewater species, found in the deep waters of the Gulf Stream, they will often feed at the surface and can been seen busting bait under birds. When fish are not visible, the common method to bring them into fly-rod range is to chum or chunk for them. Yellowfin come readily to the surface when chummed from an anchored boat. When yellowfin are hooked, expect long, deep, drag-burning runs. Fly rods of 12- and 14-weight are best suited for this fishery. They provide the lifting power necessary to pry these fish out of the depths.

Hot Spots

Although you can catch yellowfin tuna in the offshore waters of the Gulf Stream from New Jersey to the Florida Keys and throughout the Gulf of Mexico, to date, North Carolina has been the most popular fly-rod destination for yellowfin on the East Coast.

North Carolina's Outer Banks have always been a yellowfin hot spot. Yellowfin tuna are one of the most abundant fish found in the Gulf Stream, which is located about 35 miles southeast of Oregon Inlet and 35 miles east of Hatteras Inlet. The area known as the 1250 Rocks is the local hot spot; it is located at the edge of the continental shelf. Here, the water changes color as the cooler inshore waters mix with the warmer, deep blue waters of the Gulf Stream. The seams and rips formed by the blending of the two bodies of water tend to trap baitfish, and that's where you'll find the yellowfin. The fish there run from 15 to over 100 pounds and are available from mid-fall until late winter.

In the fall of 1999, Steve Hutchins landed six yellowfin tuna up to 50 pounds in one outing while fishing on Capt. Brenner Park's boat, *Smoker,* out of Oregon Inlet. Six fly-rod yellowfin in a day is quite a feat, but when you consider that all six were taken on surface poppers, that's really news! A relatively short news flash, however, if your wife breaks the fly-rod women's world record on the very same outing. Theresa Hutchins' record was 39 pounds, taken on 20-pound tippet. Less than three weeks later, she went back and broke the 16-pound class tippet record with a 16-pound yellowfin.

On another trip in the fall of 1999, also out of Oregon Inlet, Capt. Brian Horsley fished with Dickie Harris on his 55-foot *Fintastic.* They were joined by Raz Reid, a veteran bluewater fly fisher and 16-pound tippet class bluefin tuna world-record holder. The trio landed six of the nine yellowfin hooked that day. The fish ranged from 20 to 40 pounds. They fished sinking lines to drift their 2/0 to 4/0 butterfish imitations with the chum. They used 13- and 14-weight rods, but claimed that 12-weights would have worked on most of the fish.

Records

The IGFA all-tackle record yellowfin tuna weighed 388 pounds, 12 ounces. It was caught by Curt Wiesenhutter on April 1, 1977, off the Revillagigedo Islands in Mexico. Like bluefin, fly fishing for yellowfin tuna is just gaining popularity, with 9 of the 12 class tippet records having been set since 1998. On October 21, 2000, fishing out of Oregon Inlet, Theresa Hutchins broke her own world-record 20-pound tippet class with a 43-pound, 8-ounce yellowfin. In early December of 2001, again fishing off North Carolina's Outer Banks on Capt. Cliff Spencer's *Anticipation*, Theresa shattered her own 16-pound tippet record by almost 40 pounds with a 55-pound, 5-ounce monster. The very next day, Capt. Sara Gardner landed a 53-pound, 4-ounce, pending 20-pound tippet class world record. Her husband, Capt. Brian Horsley, and Raz Reid accompanied Sara on the *Sea Creature*. The group fished 13- and 14-weight rods to schools of 50- to 80-pound tuna blasting through butterfish chunks.

Current IGFA Fly Rod Records for Yellowfin

Tippet	Weight (l\bs./oz.)	Location	Angler	Date
Male				
2	3/13	Cross, Seamount, Hawaii	Kevin Nakamaru	4/6/95
4	11/14	Cabo San Lucas, Mexico	Robert Cunningham, Jr.	11/1/98
6	19/0	Gulf of Mexico, LA	Scott Harness	8/25/98
8	42/5	Maiquetia, Venezuela	A. C. Reuter	1/10/91
12	67/8	Bermuda	Jim Lopez	5/7/73
16	95/14	Carnarvon, Australia	Dr. Richard Sallie	5/22/01
20	81/9	Whakatane, New Zealand	Mark Kitteridge	2/28/99
Female				
2	Vacant			
4	Vacant			
6	6/8	Baja, Mexico	Donna Anderson	11/29/98
8	15/6	Baja, Mexico	Donna Anderson	11/29/98
12	24/12	Argus Bank, Bermuda	Mrs. Cabell Williams	6/21/01
16*	16/0	Oregon Inlet, NC	Theresa Hutchins	10/31/99
20**	43/8	Oregon Inlet, NC	Theresa Hutchins	10/21/00

* Theresa Hutchins has a pending 16-pound tippet class world record of 55 pounds, 5 ounces.

** Capt. Sara Gardner has a pending 20-pound world record of 53 pounds, 4 ounces.

Albacore (*Thunnus alalunga*)

Description

Albacore, also known as longfin tuna, can be distinguished from other tunas by their long pectoral fins, which can reach back to the second dorsal and anal fins. They are the only tuna that has a white trailing edge running along the back of the tail fin. Their backs are bluish purple and their flanks are silver, with no stripes or spots. They can exceed 50 pounds but usually run 10 to 25 pounds. Albacore have beautiful, firm white meat that is sought after by the canning industry and is marketed as "solid white" tuna.

Distribution

Albacore are found offshore in waters of 40 fathoms (240 feet) or more out to the deep-water canyons. They are a temperate species, found worldwide in tropical and warm temperate seas from 59 to 77 degrees Fahrenheit. They usually remain in tropical or warm waters, but they do make occasional migrations into colder waters as far north as Nova Scotia in search of food.

Fly Fishing

Because albacore are usually found a great distance from shore, they are generally not targeted by fly fishermen.

Records

The IGFA all-tackle world record is 88 pounds, 2 ounces and was taken off the Canary Islands on November 19, 1977, by Siegfried Dickemann. The fly-rod world record is 47 pounds, taken in the Hudson Canyon off New Jersey's coast on September 7, 1992, by Robert Lubarsky. This is the only fly-rod record taken out of the western Atlantic. Several smaller fish have been taken on fly rods off the coasts of South Africa and California.

Bigeye Tuna (*Thunnus obesus*)

Description

Bigeye tuna are similar in general appearance to yellowfins. They have a plump body, a larger head, and unusually large eyes. Their long pectoral fin reaches the second dorsal fin. Bigeye tuna found in waters of the western Atlantic are usually over 100 pounds, and they can weigh up to 400 pounds.

Distribution

Bigeye tuna can be found in the Atlantic Ocean from southern Nova Scotia down to Brazil. They are caught mainly by commercial longliners. Sportfishing for bigeyes is not common because they travel far below the surface of the water. Adult bigeyes are the deepest occurring of all tuna species, with greatest concentrations found between 150 and 250 fathoms (600 to 1,000 feet). Because of their preference for deep water and their great size, they are not targeted by flyrodders.

Hot Spots

Off Montauk, bigeyes are rarely caught inside the canyon, which is almost 70 miles from Montauk at its closest point. In New Jersey waters, a few bigeye are caught by trollers in the Hudson Canyon.

Records

The IGFA all-tackle world-record bigeye tuna weighed 392 pounds, 6 ounces and was caught by Dieter Vogel off the coast of Spain on July 25, 1996. There is only one fly-rod record of an Atlantic bigeye, a 9-pound, 14-ounce fish taken on 16-pound tippet by Christian Benazeth off Mauritania on October 23, 1991. There are several Pacific bigeye fly rod tippet records taken from Japan and Hawaii, with the largest, a 31-pound, 8-ounce fish taken on 12-pound tippet by Tomoyoshi Kagami on June 7, 1994, off Kume Island, Japan.

Part II

Hot Spots and Happy Hours

Cape Cod and the Islands

The state of Massachusetts is a saltwater flyrodder's paradise. An angler could spend a lifetime exploring the Cape and nearby islands and never fish the same water twice. Massachusetts is synonymous with striped bass; no other state can match it for size and numbers of bass. Stripers form the base on which Massachusetts has built a saltwater recreational fishery that annually generates close to $1 billion. The Cape and the islands have a long history of welcoming flyrodders, and some of the most experienced fly fishing guides on the East Coast operate here. In this re-

TOM GILMORE

A bonito off Martha's Vineyard

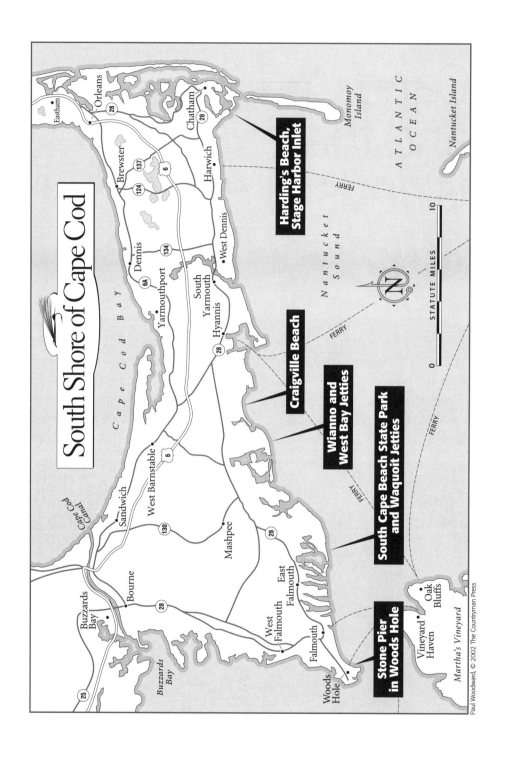

South Shore of Cape Cod

Harding's Beach, Stage Harbor Inlet

Craigville Beach

Wianno and West Bay Jetties

South Cape Beach State Park and Waquoit Jetties

Stone Pier in Woods Hole

Cape Cod Bay

Nantucket Sound

ATLANTIC OCEAN

Monomoy Island

Nantucket Island

Buzzards Bay

Martha's Vineyard

Cape Cod Canal

STATUTE MILES

0 10

Eastham

Orleans

Brewster

Chatham

Harwich

West Dennis

Dennis

Yarmouthport

South Yarmouth

Hyannis

West Barnstable

Sandwich

Mashpee

Bourne

Buzzards Bay

West Falmouth

East Falmouth

Falmouth

Woods Hole

Vineyard Haven

Oak Bluffs

FERRY

Paul Woodward, © 2002 The Countryman Press

gion, I had the pleasure of interviewing a dozen seasoned guides who have over 175 combined years of experience in targeting false albacore and bonito.

While the guides have been catching bonito as far back as they can remember, the increase in false albacore has been a more recent trend. Their consensus is that false albacore numbers have definitely increased in this area over the last 5 to 7 years. The guides' only complaint is that albies tend to displace the bonito. Bonito show in these waters first, usually around mid-July. False albacore follow around mid- to late August, when the water warms to its seasonal high. Prime albie fishing usually starts right after Labor Day and continues into early October.

The south side of the Cape around Monomoy Island, Martha's Vineyard, and Nantucket Island is generally considered to be the northern limit of the inshore tuna. Once you round Monomoy Island and head north toward Cape Cod National Seashore, the chilling influence of the waters from the Gulf of Maine are clearly noticeable. The waters along the National Seashore can be 10 degrees colder than the waters off Falmouth, setting a natural northern barrier for false albacore migration.

Cape Cod

The best false albacore fishing on the Cape occurs on the south side in the waters from Falmouth to Chatham Inlet and around Monomoy Island. These waters are nourished and fed by the tidal ponds, marshes, and bays, which harbor large quantities of bait including sand eels, silversides, peanut bunker, and blueback herring. Most of these tidal areas have jetties protecting their inlets, providing flyrodders excellent opportunities for shore-caught tuna. South shore boat anglers, in addition to targeting the mouths of inlets, can chase these speedsters along the beaches and in the nearshore rips. During prime time, albies are abundant throughout Vineyard and Nantucket Sounds, from Woods Hole to Monomoy Island and through Buzzard's Bay and Lackey's Bay. Shore anglers get good action along the south shore from the Stone Pier in Woods Hole and the Waquoit, West Bay, and Wianno Jetties, as well as along Craigville Beach and Harding's Beach.

Stone Pier in Woods Hole

For ease of access and reliability, for shore fishing the Stone Pier in Woods Hole is hard to beat. Check any fish wire from late August to early October and you will usually find daily reports of shots of false albacore or bonito from this popular area. It is probably the best location on the Cape to take a tuna from shore. This spot provides about six weeks of almost daily shore shots from late August to mid-October. Just follow the signs for the ferry in Woods Hole. As you approach the ferry, the signs will direct you to turn left on Crane Street. Instead of going to the ferry, turn right on Water Street, which takes you into Woods Hole. A few blocks down Water Street is the National Ocean & Atmosphere Administration (NOAA) ship and building on your left just before Albatross Street. The Stone Pier is right behind this building. Parking is available along the street, and from personal experience, let me warn you that the authorities take their parking meters very seriously. Due to the popularity of this tourist spot, I suggest you plan to get there early.

South Cape Beach State Park and Waquoit Jetties

Heading east from Woods Hole into Falmouth, the next area worth exploring is South Cape Beach State Park in Mashpee. From Falmouth, take Route 28 east past the Waquoit Bay Research Reservation to Red Brook Road. Turn right onto Red Brook Road and go two miles to the intersection of Great Oak Road. Turn right onto Great Oak for 2.1 miles to the sign directing you to the state park. This is a large state park, with a beautiful beach overlooking Nantucket Sound. There is plenty of public parking, with a daily in-season fee. Albies run the entire beach, but the best spots from shore are the jetties where Waquoit Bay enters Nantucket Sound to the west. If you have a kayak or canoe you can often chase them well up inside the bay. The walk to the jetty is about 1.5 miles, but at prime time it can be well worth the effort.

Continuing east into Barnstable, there are several shore locations that can provide almost daily shots at false albacore; however, with the exception of Craigville and Harding's Beaches, the parking access points are posted for town permits only. I mention them briefly for the boating angler or those that have some local friends. In many Northeast locations, the parking and beach access restrictions are eased after Labor Day, so it pays to check with local officials.

Wianno and West Bay Jetties

From Osterville, take Wianno Avenue until it dead-ends at Sea View Avenue. There is a small town lot and a series of small jetties to the east. Early morning, you can often find albies and bonito crashing through bait within casting distance of the jetties. To reach West Bay, take Sea View Avenue for two miles until it ends at the small parking area overlooking the bay. The east jetty protecting the inlet into West Bay is very fly-rod friendly and just a short walk from convenient parking. In late August through September, the bay is loaded with small silversides, and albies will often come inside this small, protected bay in search of this bait. This area is also ideal for canoe and kayak fishing. For shore fishing, the jetty is a short walk to your left. Remember to stay below the high tide line when walking past private property.

Craigville Beach

In the town of Barnstable, there is a large public beach with plenty of parking and a daily parking fee in season. From late August into early October, early mornings can provide fast and furious action on false albacore as they run the Craigville and Covell Beaches east to Squaw Island. This action can be just out of reach of shore-bound anglers; therefore, a kayak would be a good option. Craigville Beach is just a few miles south of Route 28 in Barnstable. Follow signs for Craigville Beach from Route 28, a total of 1.3 miles to the beach. This will take you to Old Stage Road, which shortly turns into Main Street and then Craigville Beach Road.

Harding's Beach, Stage Harbor Inlet in Chatham

In September, albies and bonito push bait, predominately sand eels and silversides, along the 1.5-mile stretch of Harding's Beach, from the water in front of the parking lot down to the entrance of Stage Harbor. Harding's Beach is accessed by taking Route 28 east past Route 137 for 1.5 miles and turning right on Barn Hill Road. Go three-tenths of a mile to Harding's Beach Road; follow Harding's Beach Road for 1 mile to the parking lot and beach. The lot is free to all vehicles after September 1.

Martha's Vineyard

If you get to Woods Hole or Hyannis, it's more than worth your time to grab a ferry and hit the islands. Martha's Vineyard was called "Noepe" by the Indians, which means "in the midst of the sea." The Vineyard is 5 miles off the coast of Massachusetts. At 20 miles long and 10 wide, it is the largest island off the coast of southern Massachusetts. The Woods Hole, Martha's Vineyard, and Nantucket Steamship Authority provides year-round ferry access to the island.

For many Northeast coastal flyrodders, Martha's Vineyard is Nirvana. No other location affords shore-bound anglers so many opportu-

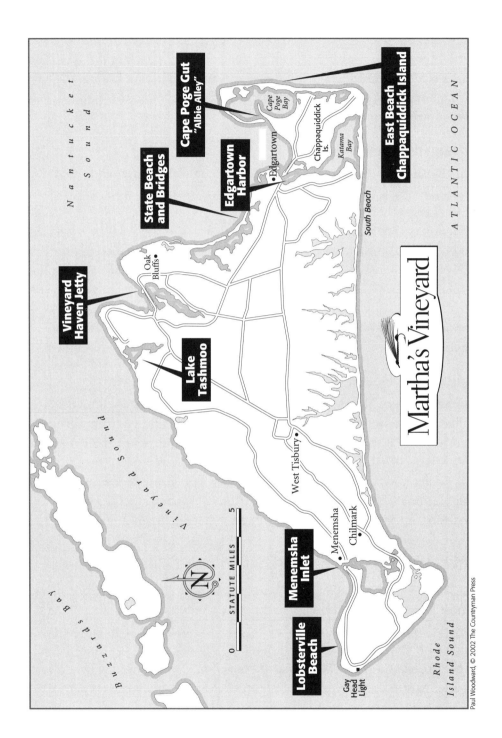

Martha's Vineyard

Nantucket Sound

Vineyard Sound

Buzzards Bay

Rhode Island Sound

ATLANTIC OCEAN

STATUTE MILES
0   5

N

Cape Poge Gut "Albie Alley"

East Beach Chappaquiddick Island

State Beach and Bridges

Edgartown Harbor

Vineyard Haven Jetty

Lake Tashmoo

Menemsha Inlet

Lobsterville Beach

Oak Bluffs

Edgartown

Chappaquiddick Is.

Cape Poge Bay

Katama Bay

South Beach

West Tisbury

Menemsha

Chilmark

Gay Head Light

nities to catch false albacore and bonito. The Vineyard is unique in that you can fish in almost any weather condition and somewhere find the right combination of tidal flow and fishable winds. In most years, bonito arrive in late July, followed by false albacore in late August or early September. The reason shore fishermen can be so successful at the Vineyard is the numerous tidal ponds, which host vast amounts of bait. The outflows of these ponds on a falling tide deliver tons of bait through narrow openings to waiting predators. In addition, false albacore will often come inside the ponds on a rising tide and chase the bait around, giving shorebound anglers excellent opportunities.

Albie Alley

"Albie Alley" might be the best place on the planet to fly fish for tuna from shore. Stretching from the entrance of Edgartown Harbor on Martha's Vineyard to Cape Poge Lighthouse on the northeast corner of Chappaquiddick Island, you can count on the Alley to provide daily shore shots at tuna.

My favorite spot along the Alley is Cape Poge Gut, which to the locals is the true Albie Alley on Chappaquiddick Island. This is a narrow opening through which all the bait and predators entering or leaving the waters of Cape Poge Bay must navigate. The Gut is only 100 yards wide, and both rising and falling water bring predators very close to shore. If you don't have access to a four-wheel-drive vehicle, try the bluffs on the North Neck of "Chappy" on an incoming tide. On incoming water, the rip sets up close to the bluff side of the Gut and brings blitzing false albacore within casting range.

To get to the North Bluff, take the *On-Time* ferry from Edgartown to Chappaquiddick. From Main Street in Edgartown, make a left on North Water Street and a right on Kelly Street to the ferry. It's a very short ride, since the opening is only 100 yards wide. Chappy residents like their privacy and have successfully thwarted any thoughts of building a bridge. Once on Chappy Point, follow Chappaquiddick Road approximately 1.2 miles to North Neck Road. This is a dirt road that comes in on the left. Take North Neck Road past the golf course to the end. There is a small fishermen's parking area on the left. Park here and take the dirt trail to the top of the bluff. There you will be treated to a spectacular panoramic view of Nantucket Sound and Cape Poge Bay and a staircase down to the Gut.

TOM GILMORE

The Cape Poge Gut, or "Albie Alley," on Chappaquiddick Island

Cape Poge and East Beach

On a falling tide, the Cape Poge Elbow side of the Gut fishes better, but you will need a four-wheel-drive vehicle and a beach permit, which you can purchase from the Trustees of the Reservation. While the Cape Poge Wildlife Refuge access to the Gut is often closed in spring and summer due to nesting piping plover (a federally endangered species), the beach is usually open by tuna time. To reach Cape Poge, take Chappaquiddick Road 2.5 miles from the ferry. As the road makes a sharp turn to the right, continue straight on the unpaved Dike Road one-half mile to the infamous Dike Bridge. The bridge has been reopened after many years of being closed to vehicle traffic. Continue over Dike Bridge to the Cape Poge gatehouse and the entrance to Cape Poge Wildlife Refuge. From here, head north (left) on the sand roads on either the Cape Poge Bay or Nantucket Sound side of the narrow sand spit known as East Beach.

Schools of albies come well up into Cape Poge Bay, chasing bait and tearing up the usually tranquil waters of this protected bay. If the boat traffic is minimal, you can gain access to them with canoe or kayak. They are not usually reachable in the main bay on foot until you get to the narrow outlet known as the Gut. This is where the waters of Cape Poge Bay mix with those of Nantucket Sound. The best bet is to drive down the sound side from the East Beach jetty to the elbow, which is marked by the Cape Poge Lighthouse. The mussel bar in front of the light is an excellent spot to try. You can safely wade about 100 feet out into the sound. From here to the Gut, which is about one-half mile south, you will find large concentrations of sand eels and silversides hugging the beach, bringing predators into fly-rod range. Remember that no matter how good East Beach looks, if you are there on a falling tide check out the Gut.

Edgartown Harbor

Another great shore spot along Albie Alley is the entrance to Edgartown Harbor. I have taken albies from the town dock as they chased bait right under my feet. You can also take the small three-car ferry across the harbor and fish Chappy Point. Parking is in the paved lot on the left. This sand beach has a steep drop-off into the channel, and it brings albies very close to the shore. There is also a sharp drop to the deep water of the channel on the harbor entrance in front of the lighthouse. Incoming water can bring the albies tight to the lighthouse beach. The harbor fishes best at first light before the boat traffic gets going.

Other shore hot spots worth trying include the jetties at the outlets of Lake Tashmoo, Sengekontacket, Lagoon, and Menemsha Ponds, and all along Lobsterville Beach.

Lake Tashmoo

Lake Tashmoo is a tidal pond on the northwest side of the island. It is famous for its "worm hatch," which occurs on the spring and early summer moon tides. During this time, striped bass cruise the shallows sucking worms off the surface, gently rolling and sipping like trout in a western lake. Tashmoo is a great location for a beginning fly fisherman to get a shot at an albacore. Although false albacore can be found crashing bait throughout the pond, the best location is the very friendly jetty at the pond's narrow outlet to Vineyard Sound. You can catch tuna here at any time, but shore-bound locals on the Vineyard prefer incoming tide at first light, and Lake Tashmoo is no exception, with the best time being the last three hours of the incoming tide. The waters of the pond are well-protected, and canoe and kayak fishing can be excellent before the boat traffic starts. If you trailer a boat, the public boat ramp on the pond is located at the end of Lake Street. From Vineyard Haven, take Franklin north to Clough Lane; turn left onto Clough, which will shortly turn into Lake Street. To reach the jetty from Vineyard Haven take either Franklin or Main Street north and turn left on Daggett Avenue. Follow Daggett until it dead-ends at a housing development; take the second dirt road on the right (Herring Creek Road) to the inlet.

State Beach and the Bridges

State Beach is located on Beach Road between Oak Bluffs and Edgartown. Behind the beach and road are the bait-rich waters of Sengekontacket Pond. The pond has two openings to Nantucket Sound and both are protected with jetties. The smaller opening, Little Bridge, is toward Oak Bluffs and the larger opening, Anthers, or Big Bridge, is toward Edgartown. False albacore run the beach near these openings from first light until the boat traffic spreads them out. Get there at first light if you want a shore shot from this popular spot.

Vineyard Haven Jetty

The jetty facing Vineyard Harbor, just outside Lagoon Pond, is another hot spot for bonito and false albacore. This spot fishes best from shore near the top of the tide and can be especially productive if you have

DAVE W. SKOK

Tom Rapone with an albie from Lobsterville Beach, Martha's Vineyard

northwest winds, which push bait against the jetty and bring marauding tuna within reach of fly fishermen. The jetty is one-half mile east of the Vineyard Haven Ferry Dock. Take Beach Road across the Lagoon Pond drawbridge and turn left into the Eastville Beach parking area. The jetty is a short walk to your left. There is a public boat ramp in Lagoon Pond that provides good access to Vineyard Haven Harbor. The launch also provides excellent access to some of the better nearshore fishing areas. East and West Chop are just minutes from Lagoon Pond, as are some of the more famous rips that lie between Vineyard Haven and Woods Hole.

Lobsterville, Gay Head

Lobsterville Beach is a world-famous fly fishing destination for striped bass and bluefish. Since the late 1980s, I have made annual visits on the new moon in June to fish for striped bass that come into the shallows of Vineyard Sound to feed on the large concentrations of sand eels and herring that hug the beach to avoid predation. From late August well into October, albies run the beach from Dogfish Bar to the Menemsha jetties. Anywhere along the beachfront can produce good action, but I have had the best action fishing from mid-bowl east to the jetty.

Lobsterville Beach is accessed by taking South Road to Lobsterville Road. Turn right on Lobsterville Road and continue for seven-tenths of a mile. As the road bends to the right, you'll see Vineyard Sound on your left. Look for a small parking area on the left side of the road adjacent to the beach. From the parking area, Dogfish Bar is to your left or west about one mile. To your right or east, you have about 3 miles of fishing in the bowl all the way to the jetties at Menemsha.

Menemsha

The jetties at the outflow of Menemsha Pond rank as one of the most consistent shore spots on the island. Many bonito and false albacore derby winners have been taken from these jetties, including two 12-pound beauties by Dave Skok that took top honors in 2000 and 2001. To reach the inlet to Menemsha Pond, continue past the Lobsterville parking lot and turn left on West Basin Road. The road ends at the pond. There is a public boat launch and parking for cars and trailers. This gives you access to the west or Lobsterville jetty on Menemsha Inlet. Incoming tide often brings false albacore inside the inlet between the jetties and back inside the pond. On outgoing tide, they usually feed off the mouth of the inlet, often just outside of the range of jetty jocks.

While both jetties fish well for albacore and bonito, I favor the Lobsterville side. It is generally less crowded than the Menemsha side, and if the tuna go back into the pond the Lobsterville side gives foot anglers better access. To reach the Menemsha side, take North Road west to Basin Road, turn right on Basin Road and take it to the end, where you'll find a large public parking lot. Menemsha has fine dining and a great sunset over Vineyard Sound.

Boat Hot Spots

Boat fishermen do exceptionally well fishing the outlets of all the salt ponds on the island. The waters between Cape Cod and Martha's Vineyard provide some terrific nearshore fishing. The bottom of Nantucket Sound is largely sand and the current builds sandbars or mounds. The bottom averages between 15 and 50 feet, but can go from as deep as 70 feet to as shallow as 5 or 6 feet. The water running over these sand structures increases in speed, causing tremendous tidal rips. These rips funnel and disorient the bait, providing excellent opportunities for predators to find an easy meal.

Regular hot spots include: East and West Chop, Hedge Fence, Middle Ground, L'Hommedieu, and Succonesset Shoals. Bonito and albies come

Menemsha Inlet, Martha's Vineyard

to the Vineyard from the east, showing first at Hooters, which is a 6-mile run south from Wasque Point.

Nantucket

Nantucket was once the whaling capital of the world. Today, tourism is the economic base for this spectacularly beautiful island. Nantucket derives its name from an Indian word meaning "faraway land" or "land far out to sea." It lies about 30 miles south of Cape Cod. Because of the greater distance and longer ferry ride from Woods Hole and Hyannis, Nantucket is not as popular with the fly fishing fraternity as Martha's Vineyard. It does have several good fly shops and a number of excellent guides. The island is considerably smaller than the Vineyard, being approximately 4 miles long and 14 miles wide. Islanders take intense pride in preserving their open space and historic sites. Over 35 percent of the island is permanently protected conservation lands. Nantucket has more buildings listed on the National Register of Historic Places than Boston, Plymouth, or Salem, Massachusetts. You will find no traffic lights or fast-food restaurants on this island.

Nantucket is closer to the Gulf Stream than the Vineyard and it can provide tremendous shore and boat fishing for false albacore and bonito. Like the Vineyard, Nantucket's prime false albacore fishing is from approximately Labor Day into the first week of October. If you plan to fish Nantucket from shore, locals recommend a beach buggy to access the better shore spots. If you choose to bring your own vehicle, be sure to make your ferry reservations well in advance. You can also rent an over-sand vehicle with beach permits on the island. Bonito used to be the main inshore tuna in the waters surrounding the island, but in the last six or seven years, Nantucket has seen a tremendous increase in the number of false albacore, and they are now the dominant inshore tuna.

Get to the Point

Once on Nantucket Island, the rule for chasing tuna is "get to the Point!" Far and away the two best shore locations for false albacore are Great and Eel Points, with Great Point being the guides' unanimous choice.

Great Point

Year in and year out, the Internet reports from Jeff and Lynn Heyer at Cross Rip Outfitters and Bill Pew of Bill Fisher's Tackle cite shore anglers being treated to spectacular runs of albies all along both sides of Great

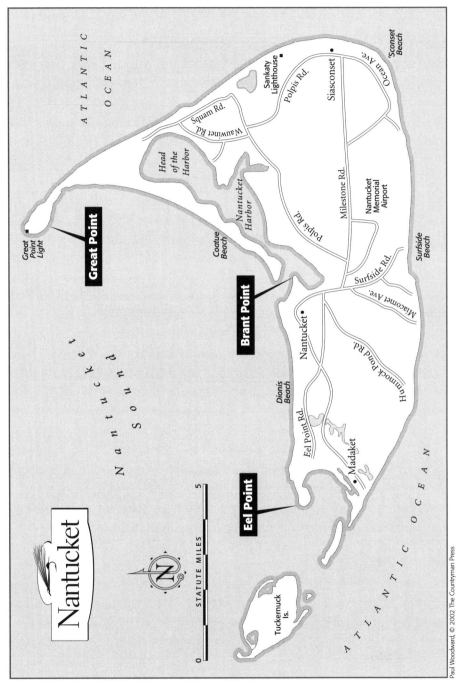

Nantucket

Great Point
Great Point Light

Brant Point

Eel Point

Eel Point Rd.
Dionis Beach
Madaket
Nantucket
Hummock Pond Rd.
Miacomet Ave.
Surfside Rd.
Surfside Beach
Nantucket Memorial Airport
Milestone Rd.
Polpis Rd.
Siasconset
Ocean Ave.
'Sconset Beach
Polpis Rd.
Sankaty Lighthouse
Wauwinet Rd.
Squam Rd.
Head of the Harbor
Nantucket Harbor
Coatue Beach

Tuckernuck Is.

Nantucket Sound

ATLANTIC OCEAN

ATLANTIC OCEAN

N

STATUTE MILES
0 5

Paul Woodward, © 2002 The Countryman Press

Point. Bill feels that when conditions are right, Great Point is probably the best spot in Massachusetts for a shore angler to accomplish a Cape Cod Slam (false albacore or bonito plus a bass and bluefish in one day). While my buddies on the Vineyard would be willing to bet even money on Menemsha or the Gut, that is still high praise, and I wouldn't go to Nantucket without giving Great Point an honest shot.

The point is located on the northeast corner of Nantucket Island. It is actually shaped like a large fishhook with the point jutting way out into Nantucket Sound and the barb coming down toward the harbor. Three conservation groups now protect over 1,600 acres and almost 18 miles of shoreline. The largest tract is Coskata-Coatue Wildlife Refuge, which totals 1,117 acres and is owned and managed by the Trustees of the Reservation.

The best fishing is at The Galls and Great Point itself. To fish the point, you will need a 4x4 and a permit from the Trustees. They have maps of the 30 miles of over-sand vehicle trails and an air pump at the Wauwinet gatehouse. Access is from the Nantucket rotary, by taking Polpis Road for 6 miles to Wauwinet Road. Turn left on Wauwinet Road and continue to the gatehouse.

Eel Point

Eel Point is another constant producer that is always worth a look, especially early in the morning before the boat traffic gets going. It has a deep channel that comes within 10 feet of the beach where false albacore and bonito run within easy casting distance of shore anglers. Eel Point is another shore location where it is possible to land a beach grand slam. To access Eel Point from town, take Madaket Road and Eel Point Road to the end.

Brant Point and Nantucket Harbor

Built in 1746, Brant Point Lighthouse is the second oldest lighthouse in America. Only Boston's Beacon Light is older. Brant Point and the harbor jetties produce occasional shots of false albacore in the early morning hours. Because of the ease of access (you can bike to the light from downtown), it is certainly worth a shot.

Boat Hot Spots

Consistent boat fishing can be had off Great and Eel Points and from Smith's Point over to Eel Point. Lynne Heyer at Cross Rip Outfitters reports that the small channel at Smith's Point can fish very well on a dropping tide, but the channel can get so crowded during peak season that it often looks like Boca Grande Pass during the tarpon run.

Naturals and Their Imitations

The most abundant baitfish on the Cape and its islands are sand eels, followed by silversides. In recent years, the Cape and Martha's Vineyard have been seeing an increasing number of peanut bunker. Bay anchovy, which are a very important baitfish from Rhode Island south to the Outer Banks of North Carolina, rarely occur in the waters of the south Cape and islands. The most popular patterns used to match sand eels and silversides are small, sparse Clousers and Deceivers. Favorite colors would include all-white and white with a green, olive, or chartreuse back. One very productive local pattern, developed by Capt. Jamie Boyle, is the Bonito Bunny. Dave Skok, one of the best shore anglers in the Northeast and a regular on the Martha's Vineyard Derby leader board, has had tremendous success with a pattern he originally developed for skipjack tuna called the Mushmouth. Epoxy patterns like Bob Popovics's Surf Candy produce well everywhere there are small translucent baitfish like silversides or bay anchovy.

Rhode Island's Breachways and Connecticut's Rips

11

Rhode Island, the smallest state in the union, is aptly nicknamed the Ocean State. With over 400 miles of shoreline, it's a flyrodder's paradise. Rhode Island offers three principal areas to target false albacore: the South Shore beaches and breachways, the waters of Narragansett Bay, and Block Island.

The Rhody Breachways

For shore fishing, my favorite section and one of the Northeast's premier fly fishing destinations, is the South Shore and its breachways from Watch Hill to Point Judith. This area has it all, including rocky points, long sandy beaches, and vast tidal salt ponds. A number of these ponds have openings, locally known as breachways, lined by stone jetties. These salt ponds are nurseries for a wide variety of baitfish, and the breachways serve as funnels for a vast exchange of tidal waters between the ponds and Block Island Sound. The Rhody Breachways have often treated me to a false albacore or two, and the breachway regulars have had some spectacular double-digit fish days.

One September evening, while giving a saltwater program to a local Trout Unlimited chapter, I was asked where I would fish for false albacore the coming weekend. I replied that my choice would be the Rhody Breachways. After the program, one of the members asked me for directions to the breachways. I gave him directions to Weekapaug and Quonochontaug Breachways and suggested that he try them on an incoming

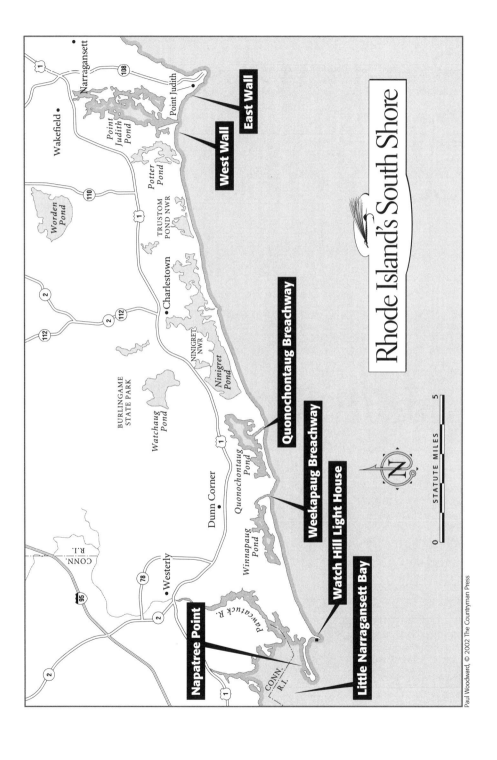

Rhode Island's South Shore

Narragansett

Wakefield •

Point Judith Pond

Point Judith

West Wall

East Wall

Potter Pond

TRUSTOM POND NWR

Worden Pond

Charlestown •

NINIGRET NWR

Ninigret Pond

BURLINGAME STATE PARK

Watchaug Pond

Quonochontaug Pond

Dunn Corner •

Quonochontaug Breachway

Weekapaug Breachway

Winnapaug Pond

• Westerly

CONN R.I.

Pawcatuck R.

Watch Hill Light House

Napatree Point

Little Narragansett Bay

CONN. R.I.

N

STATUTE MILES

0   5

Paul Woodward, © 2002 The Countryman Press

tide. He was a fly fishing novice, and as I knew how difficult it might be to catch a false albacore from shore, I gave him several of my flies and suggested he try a nearby cove for schoolie striped bass if the albies weren't cooperating. Monday morning, I received the following e-mail: "Tom, thanks a million, it was just like you said! We fished Weekapaug Saturday on the incoming tide and hooked over a dozen albies, landing seven. Boy, do they fight! Sunday, they didn't show at Weekapaug, so we went to 'Quonnie.' When we arrived, fish were busting everywhere. We hooked a bunch and landed five. On the way back we stopped at the cove. Wow! I never saw so many birds and bass. We lost count of the number of fish that we hooked and landed. Thanks a million! PS: Where would you suggest I fish this weekend?" I can't tell you how many times I hit the Rhody Breachways following this report, trying to duplicate his two days of fishing without anywhere near that kind of success. Can you imagine how he would have done if I had told him about the West Wall at Point Judith?

The West Wall

While all of the Rhode Island breachways get good shots of false alba-core, the West Wall at Point Judith is my first choice. Over the last few

TOM GILMORE

The West Wall

years, the West Wall has been the most consistent shore spot in Rhode Island for false albacore, and it certainly ranks as one of the best shore spots on the East Coast to target inshore tuna. This breakwater protects the west side of the entrance to Point Judith Harbor, also known as the Harbor of Refuge. The Wall reaches out over a mile into Block Island Sound and has deep water on both sides. You can fish it with the wind in almost any direction, and false albacore will show on both the "inside" and "outside" of the Wall. The harbor holds tons of baitfish, mostly silversides and peanut bunker, and this area can draw enormous schools of predators.

During the fall of 2000, flyrodders reported almost daily blitzes of albies feeding on silversides and peanut bunker through September and into early October. During this period, it was not uncommon for veteran flyrodders to have a dozen hook-ups a day, even when fish were not showing on top. Several anglers reported grand slams (a bass, bluefish, and false albacore in one day) from the Wall. Grand slams are always quite an accomplishment when fishing from shore. The Wall tends to fish better with moving water on either side of high tide. Fish tend to feed the last three hours of the incoming tide then shut off when the tide slackens. They resume in earnest when the current picks up during the dropping tide.

To reach the West Wall from Route 1 in South Kingstown, take Succotash Road and follow signs for Jerusalem. After about 1.2 miles you will pass Captain Jack's on the right. This is where the locals go for fresh seafood—great food and good prices. At 1.6 miles the East Matunuck State Beach will appear on your right; continue on for a total of 2.3 miles from Route 1 until Succotash Road makes a sharp left. At this spot there is a small private road known as Beach Row on your right. Make the left hand turn and park on the left side, across the street from Skip's or Jim's Dock. After you park, walk back to Beach Row, and go over the dunes to the West Wall.

The East Wall

Across the harbor is the East Wall in Point Judith near the lighthouse. It is also referred to as the Jetty at Camp Cronin. The East Wall or Breachway, while not as long as the West Wall, gives you access to deep water and good fly fishing in most wind conditions.

From US Route 1 in South Kingstown, take the exit for Route 108 south and Point Judith. Follow 108 south for 4.5 miles to the stop sign at the intersection of Ocean Road. Turn right onto Ocean Road and continue for six-tenths of a mile to the entrance for the Camp Cronan Fishing Area. Turn right onto the dirt road; the Point Judith Lighthouse will be

TOM GILMORE

Weekapaug Breachway

on your left. As you continue, the road turns right and the jetty will appear on your left. This is a public fishing area, which is maintained by the Rhode Island Fish & Wildlife Department.

Weekapaug Breachway

Weekapaug Breachway is a favorite fly-rod spot for locals and visiting anglers alike. Many a Northeast grand slam has come from both the east and west jetties that protect this narrow inlet, which exchanges the waters of Winnapaug Pond and Block Island Sound. Mid-September through early October is the prime time to target tuna from the rocks. This popular location has easy access, parking on both sides of the breachway, and a street bridge that gives easy access to either jetty.

From Route 1 in Westerly, take the exit for Weekapaug/Misquamicut Beach. Continue for 1 mile and the breachway appears on your right. This area is all privately owned. Continue a total of 1.4 miles from Route 1 to the bridge at Atlantic Avenue. There is access to public fishing with parking lots on both sides of the breachway.

Quonochontaug Breachway

Quonochontaug Breachway, better known as "Quonnie," funnels enormous amounts of water and bait from the vast tidal pond to the waters

TOM GILMORE

Matt Toomey fighting albie from Quonochontaug Breachway

of Block Island Sound. It delivers more than twice the flow of Weekapaug Breachway, so it has a greater chance of drawing migrating predators. The pond itself is a local favorite for bluefish and striped bass. From the east jetty, you can have shots from the mouth of the inlet all the way inside to the pocket at the bend, which often harbors great quantities of bait.

From Route 1, take the exit for West Beach Road in Charlestown. Follow West Beach Road for 2 miles until it turns into a dirt road. The Breachway is on your left. You can continue for another two-tenths of a mile to the dead-end at Quonochontaug Pond and a public boat launch. Access to Quonnie can be difficult in the summer, but during September access improves. At the 1.8-mile mark coming in, you pass a small three-car parking area on the left. This has a small sign that says private parking June to Labor Day. In the fall, you can park here and take the trail on the right to the beach (the sign says "Show Beach Pass"). Once on the beach, walk toward the west, or right, and this will take you to the east jetty at Quonnie.

Charlestown Breachway is a terrific striper spot, but it generally doesn't get the number of false albacore that the other breachways do. The ebb in these breachways starts about two and a half hours after high tide on the beach. Due to the powerful exchange of water, most breachway regulars prefer to fish sinking or sink-tip fly lines to get the fly down a foot or more below the surface.

In early October, as the water starts to cool, the peanut bunker start to leave the Rhode Island salt ponds in massive schools. This migration usually generates massive feeding frenzies. One angler reported a school of peanut bunker 100 yards long, 40 yards wide, and 4 feet deep on the inside of one of the inlets. With Rhode Island's clear water, from high vantage points like the breachway jetties you can often see false albacore race great distances to attack your offering. I can guarantee from personal experience that this is an incredible visual fishing experience.

Watch Hill, Napatree Point, and Little Narragansett Bay

At the far western end of Rhode Island's South Shore lies Napatree Beach and Point, a 1½-mile sand spit that separates Little Narragansett Bay from Block Island Sound. Napatree once had about 50 vacation homes, until the storm of 1938 cut it in half and demolished the structures. It is now a state park, and it offers excellent fishing on both the sound and bay sides. Napatree regulars generally target bass and bluefish, but on many late September and early October mornings, I have seen false albacore running the length of this beach crashing through balls of bay anchovies in 4 feet of water. Just off the beach, the nearshore Watch Hill rips provide some of the best grand slam action on the Rhode Island coast.

My first shallow-water false albacore experience took place on the flats of Little Narragansett Bay behind Napatree Point. I had fished the Watch Hill rips from my fishing crony Matt Toomey's 17-foot Boston Whaler for several days. On that October morning, northeast winds of up to 35 knots kept us tucked up inside Napatree Point. We had decided to fish at first light, searching the shallows for bass that had been munching on silversides all night under the safety of that October new moon. We were quietly inching our way toward the harbor when Matt hollered that he had spotted albies. He hit the throttle and spun the boat in the direction of the busting fish, but they were gone in an instant. I was convinced that he must have seen bluefish that he mistook for albies, since we were over a mile inside the point in less than 3 feet of water. Just then, albies erupted 50 feet off the stern, and there was no mistaking their powerful explosions. I got lucky. My cast was right on target, and the fly was taken at full speed by an albie that would later push my Boga grip to over 12 pounds. My line sliced through the shallows and headed straight for Stonington, Connecticut. That fish never changed direction; it just kept tearing off line until it exposed backing that had never seen the light of day. That was the only false albacore we took that day, but I will never forget the slicing sound my line made as it literally ripped the shallow waters of Little Narragansett Bay in half.

To reach Watch Hill and Napatree Point, take I-95 to Exit 1, Route 78 East. Go through the light at the end of the ramp and continue down Watch Hill Road for about 2.5 miles to downtown Watch Hill. The road changes to Bay Street in town. Park in the lot next to the harbor on your right.

Narragansett

Farther north the waters related to Narragansett Bay provide excellent boat fishing for false albacore. The shoreline heading north in Rhode Island changes dramatically as the sandy beaches of the South Shore quickly turn into what could easily be mistaken for the rocky coast of Maine. This is an area of rock cliffs, big surf, and white water—striper surf. While this area is famous for its striper fishing, shore striper hot spots like Hazard and Newton Avenues in Narragansett do give up their fair share of false albacore. This rocky coast area requires wearing corkers over your footwear, and I would advise never fishing these waters alone.

One of the best shore spots on Rhode Island's North Shore is the water of Sachuest Bay. It's not uncommon for false albacore to run Sachuest or Second Beach chasing the bait out to the deep water on the west side of Sachuest Point. Ample parking and restroom accommodations can be found at the Sachuest National Wildlife Refuge. The point is an easy 10-minute walk, and by taking the westernmost trail, you might spot breaking fish along the deep water on the way out.

Narragansett boating hot spots include Brenton Point, in front of the Cliff Walk in Newport, and Sakonnet Point and Harbor near Little Compton.

To reach Sachuest Point, take route 138a east out of Newport into Middletown where it turns into Purgatory Road, as you continue east this will turn into Sachuest Point Road, which parallels Second Beach. Follow Sachuest Point Road to the NWR parking lot. Take the westernmost hiking trail, which overlooks Second Beach and Sachuest Bay to the point.

Block Island

Block Island is located about 15 miles east of Montauk, New York, and 12 miles south of Galilee, Rhode Island. Bonito arrive at Block Island around the first of August, followed a few weeks later by false albacore. Albies are the first to leave this area and are usually gone by mid-October. Block Island is host to numerous shore hot spots for bass and bluefish, but for false albacore, none can match the entrance to Great Salt Pond by the U.S. Coast Guard station. The Coast Guard channel into New Harbor has easy access and it is definitely one of the best places in the Northeast to fly fish for bonito and false albacore.

The harbor is not a true estuary habitat and it doesn't get the vast amounts of spawning bait that the other Rhode Island salt ponds do. It does get large quantities of silversides, which are the most important baitfish for false albacore in the cut. The Coast Guard Cut usually offers daily shots, but you may have to put in your time. Increase your odds by fishing moving water; early morning is often the most productive time. There is public access to Beans Point, but the Coast Guard side of the cut usually provides better fishing, as sand eels and silversides hug the water's edge. Through the crystal-clear water, you can see the albies fly by, literally crashing through bait right at your feet. If boat traffic is light, you might try fishing the harbor from a canoe or kayak, as false albacore and bonito often chase bait well up into the shallows. The cut is just a short cab ride from the ferry or the airport on the island.

Year-round car and passenger ferries run from Point Judith, Rhode Island to Block Island, and a car and passenger ferry runs from June to September out of New London, Connecticut. Summer passenger ferries run out of Providence and Newport, Rhode Island and Montauk, New York. To reach the Point Judith ferry from US Route 1 in South Kingstown, take Route 108 south for approximately 4 miles until you see the sign for the ferry on your right. This is Galilee Escape Road. Turn right and follow the signs. The ferry is about 1 mile from where Galilee ends at Great Island Road. Point Judith has a large commercial harbor with a fleet of trawlers and several fish-packing plants. While there are several charter boats in the area, fly fishing has yet to catch on.

Connecticut

Connecticut is famous for its nearshore rips at the entrance to Long Island Sound, which it shares bragging rights to with New York State. At the mouth of the sound and along the inner line of reefs and islands from Orient Point, New York to Watch Hill, Rhode Island there is some of the most consistent striped bass, bluefish, and false albacore fishing in this tri-state area. Most false albacore stay in the eastern end of Long Island

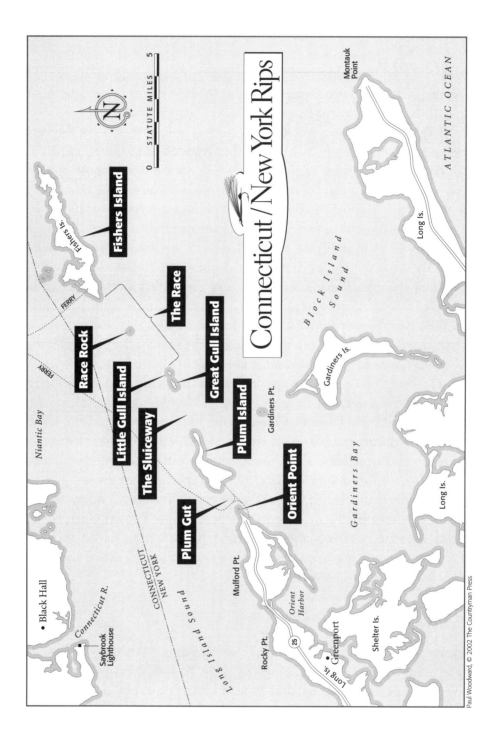

Connecticut / New York Rips

STATUTE MILES

0   5

Black Hall

Niantic Bay

Connecticut R.

Saybrook Lighthouse

CONNECTICUT
NEW YORK

Long Island Sound

Fishers Island

Fishers Is.

FERRY

FERRY

Race Rock

The Race

Little Gull Island

Great Gull Island

The Sluiceway

Plum Island

Gardiners Pt.

Plum Gut

Orient Point

Mulford Pt.

Rocky Pt.

Orient Harbor

Greenport

25

Long Is.

Shelter Is.

Gardiners Bay

Gardiners Is.

Block Island Sound

Long Is.

Long Is.

Montauk Point

ATLANTIC OCEAN

Paul Woodward, © 2002 The Countryman Press

Sound near the mouth, feeding along the rip lines. But some fish move west following bait as far back into the sound as Stratford and Fairfield, Connecticut. Several well-known western sound shore locations like Penfield Reef, Jennings Beach, the rip by the cannons at Compo Beach, and the mouth of the Housatonic, produce well for bass and bluefish and, on occasion, do give up a false albacore or two. Connecticut albie chasers should remember that, all things being equal, your odds increase the farther east you go in the sound.

The most consistent Connecticut shore spot in recent years has been the Millstone Nuclear Power Plant in Waterford, Connecticut. The powerful flow of warm water discharged from the plant is a fish magnet, attracting great quantities of bait and often school after school of feeding predators, including the inshore tunas and Spanish mackerel. When false albacore are running, the Millstone can draw a crowd and it can be difficult to find an opening to fish from shore. Currently, access to the plant is closed because of heightened security after the tragedy of September 11, 2001. As a result, shore-bound flyrodders in the area should focus their attention on the Rhode Island Breachways, which are about a one-hour car ride east of the Millstone Power Plant.

Nearshore Rips

Nearshore rips like the Race, Plum Gut, and Sluiceway contain some of the strongest tidal flows on the East Coast and provide excellent conditions for false albacore blitzes. The rips are powerful funnels that deliver immense quantities of bait to hungry predators that stage in these food factories during the fall to feed before their long migration south. Although these rips provide excellent fishing, they can be treacherous for boaters, as there are numerous rock outcroppings at, or just under, the surface that have claimed their share of motor parts. Fishing this area requires someone at the wheel who is constantly alert for rocks, ferries, sailboats, trollers, and even an occasional submarine from the New London Naval Station. Before setting out in your own boat, I strongly recommend that you spend some time on these waters with one of the local experts.

The surrounding islands provide some of the most important tern-nesting habitat in the world, including the largest breeding colony of roseate terns in North America and one of the largest colonies of common terns in the tri-state region. These large concentrations of terns and gulls can be a tremendous help in locating fish. It's not uncommon to spot clouds of these birds from miles away. However, if birds are not showing, you often can score by positioning your boat just up-current from the rip line and holding it there by stemming the tide with the motor. From this position, anglers can then cast down and across the rip, and fish will most likely nail the fly as it speeds up on the swing. While many anglers will frown on letting the fly just hang in the current at the end of a drift, it will often produce violent strikes. This is an excellent method for getting a novice into some fish.

Naturals and Their Imitations

The predominant entrees on the false albacore's menu in southern New England are bay anchovy and silversides. With the recent restrictions on bunker boats in Long Island Sound, peanut bunker are becoming a very important part of this region's food chain. In early September, there is a huge push of bay anchovy into the rips. Literally millions of tiny bay anchovy form schools so dense that the local guides refer to them as clouds or stains of bait. Right on their heals are blitzing pods of false albacore. For the next few weeks, the bait and false albacore continue to build, with

TOM GILMORE

The author deep into the backing on the Connecticut Rips

the peak time being from around mid-September until mid-October. If the weather holds, the peak can last until the end of October.

Basic fly patterns such as Clousers and Deceivers in the size and shape of the predominant bait are often all you need for fishing the rips. The fish don't have much time to scrutinize your offering in the fast-moving water. On days when albies are being selective, epoxy patterns like the Surf Candies are very popular. For the shallower inshore areas, flies that closely resemble the bait are preferred. In addition to Surf Candies, local patterns like Rhody Flat Wings, Rhody Chovies, and Johnny's Angels produce well. A more recent addition to the regional arsenal of albie-killers is the Mushmouth, which can be tied in different sizes and colors to create an excellent match for bay anchovy and silversides. Another favorite is an all-white Bonito Bunny, a rabbit-fir pattern developed by Martha's Vineyard guide Capt. Jamie Boyle. Increasing numbers of anglers in this region are using flies with weighted heads to achieve the jigging action that makes the Clouser Deep Minnow so effective. Cone heads are being added to Bunny flies, and Popovics's Deep Candies and Jiggies have gained increased popularity in the region.

The South Shore of Long Island and New Jersey's Jetty Country

12

Long Island

It All Starts at the End—Montauk Point

When Long Islanders refer to the End, they are referring to the east end of the south fork of Long Island, Montauk Point. The point juts well out into the Atlantic Ocean and all the predators and prey coming out of Long Island and Block Island Sounds must round it before heading south

Montauk Point

TOM GILMORE

or offshore for the winter. Montauk is one of the most famous aquatic food funnels and game fish staging areas on the planet.

There is a sign on the way to this fishing hub that reads: "Welcome to Montauk, Fishing Capital of the World." More IGFA world records have come from Montauk than any other place on the East Coast. Montauk is home to famous fall feeding frenzies of striped bass, bluefish, and false albacore. Under the Montauk Lighthouse may just be the best shore spot in the Northeast for trophy bass. Offshore, there is a great tuna and shark fishery. In recent years, the popularity of the fall false albacore run here has captured the attention of flyrodders from around the globe. On more than one fall weekend I have seen as many as 50 boats flyrodding for false albacore right out in front of the lighthouse.

False albacore start to arrive at the Point in late August and stay through late October. Usually, the albie blitzes start right after Labor Day, and as autumn progresses, they continue to build. Montauk's albacore season peaks the last two weeks in September through the first two weeks of October. The fish will remain until the water temperature drops into the low 50s, which is usually in late October.

While always a popular fishing destination for surfcasters and charter boats, fly fishing at the End was slow to take hold. In the late 1980s and early 1990s, there were few local guides who specialized in fly fishing, and fewer still who targeted false albacore. By and large, fly fishing for false albacore at Montauk was overlooked until Capt. Paul Dixon opened up his To the Point Charters and popularized this great fishery.

Dixon and most of the guides I interviewed from this region say they've seen a definite increase in the number of false albacore over the last seven or eight years. They are also seeing an increase in the numbers of juvenile menhaden since commercial netting was banned in Long Island Sound. While false albacore love these little peanut bunker, the bait that has made the Montauk fishery so popular is the bay anchovy. False albacore will corral these tiny baitfish into tight bait balls. The bay anchovy is a very weak-swimming bait. Once the albies have them balled up on top, these little creatures have little recourse but to huddle together, and they take quite a beating. False albacore will tear through these surface schools and continue to surface feed, giving fly-rod anglers excellent opportunities to hook up.

Dixon describes two distinct patterns of feeding that false albacore use on these bait balls. The first pattern is when the albies seem to get in perfect formation and speed through the bait ball, turning on their sides.

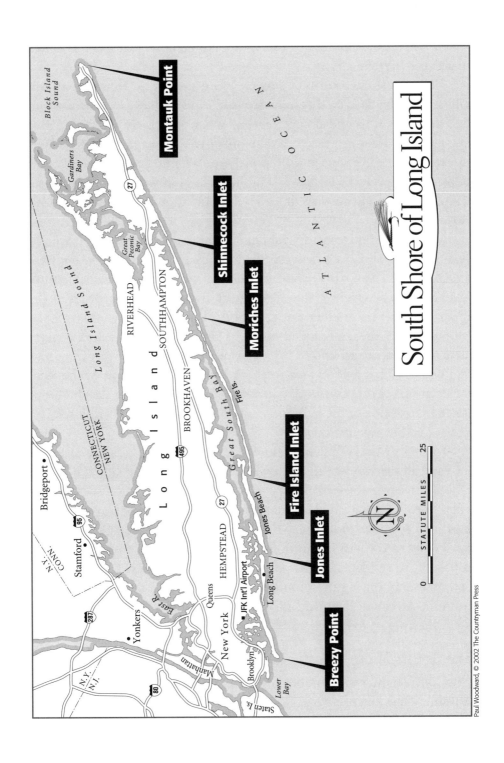

South Shore of Long Island

Montauk Point

Shinnecock Inlet

Moriches Inlet

Fire Island Inlet

Jones Inlet

Breezy Point

Block Island Sound

Gardiners Bay

Great Peconic Bay

ATLANTIC OCEAN

RIVERHEAD

SOUTHHAMPTON

BROOKHAVEN

Long Island Sound

CONNECTICUT
NEW YORK

Long Island

Great South Bay

Fire Is.

HEMPSTEAD

Jones Beach

Long Beach

JFK Int'l Airport

Queens

New York

Brooklyn

Manhattan

East R.

Yonkers

Stamford

Bridgeport

N.Y.
CONN.

N.Y.
N.J.

Staten Is.

Lower Bay

95

287

80

27

495

27

N

STATUTE MILES
0   25

Paul Woodward, © 2002 The Countryman Press

Rather than picking off individual baits, they cut, slice, and rip through the entire school. You can actually hear the sizzle as they tear through the water. When albies are feeding this way, Dixon reports that it is very tough to get them to take a fly.

The second method is a slower, more deliberate feeding pattern, which could be described as more trout-like. The albies stay with the bait ball and move up and down to feed. When albies are feeding in this manner they are much easier to take on a fly. You just need to drop your fly into the feeding zone and keep it there. When fishing in these conditions, Dixon prefers to fish a fly that has lots of movement on a slow retrieve. He recommends flies like a Fly Fir Surf Candy, or Bob Lindquist's Royal Anchovy.

At the East End, most flyrodding for false albacore is done by boat. Just offshore, about a mile west of Montauk Point, are Shagwong Reef and associated rips. This excellent ablie hot spot is easily accessible from Lake Montauk Marina. It doesn't get near as much fishing pressure as the Point does. Shore anglers can get good shots from the jetties at Lake Montauk and down along Gin Beach to Shagwong Point. Beach buggies are a common site around Montauk, especially for anglers targeting bass and bluefish. It is a good idea to check permit requirements at the local tackle shops. At this writing, you need a New York State Beach Permit for the north side of the lighthouse and a Suffolk County Permit for Gin Beach and Shagwong Point.

To get to Montauk Point, take the Long Island Expressway to Route 27 East, all the way out to the town of Montauk. This is about a 2½- to 3-hour drive from New York City. The point is 5 miles east of town. A few miles north of town is Lake Montauk or Montauk Harbor. To access the East Jetty on the harbor from Montauk Point State Park, take Lake Drive for 3 miles to the parking lot in front of the jetty and Gin Beach. This lot is posted for residents of East Hampton, but often these restrictions are enforced only during the summer months. For access to the West Jetty from the Montauk Highway, take West Lake Drive 3 miles to the public lot at the base of the jetty.

The South Shore of Long Island

Once the fish migration rounds Montauk Point, both prey and predators continue their journey along Long Island's South Shore. From Montauk to Brooklyn, the South Shore has over one hundred miles of barrier beaches, which separate the Atlantic Ocean from the back bays. There are five major inlets that cut through the barrier islands, and these inlets

The author with a bonito from Long Island Sound

exchange large quantities of water and bait between the numerous shallow back bays and the ocean. These bait-filled inlets are magnets for migrating predators and offer great shots at false albacore.

Shinnecock Inlet

Heading back west from Montauk Point, the first inlet you come to is Shinnecock Inlet. This inlet is an excellent shore albie hot spot and a very popular fly-rod destination. The inlet has a huge draw of water, exchanging the waters of Shinnecock Bay with the Atlantic Ocean. In the fall, concentrations of baitfish hug the rock jetties that line the inlet in hope of avoiding predation. The water is very clean and clear, and from a vantage point up on the rocks, strikes are often visible, even when blind casting. Shinnecock does not get the numbers of fish that Montauk gets, but the inlet brings them within a shore angler's reach.

While both the east and west jetties fish well, the hands-down favorite for flyrodders targeting false albacore is the east jetty. False albacore tend to run along this jetty in search of prey. Back inside the east jetty, there is a fly-rod-friendly beach, which can give you grand slam opportunities for false albacore, striped bass, and bluefish. Situated on both sides of the inlet are Suffolk County parks. During the summer season, the park on the east side of the inlet is restricted to county residents. Nonresidents are required to purchase a Suffolk County Tourist Green Key Card to park in the county parking lot. From there, it is a short walk to the jetty. If you have an over-sand vehicle, the card allows you to drive to the jetty. To obtain the Green Key Card, which currently costs $35 per year, write the Suffolk County Department of Parks, P.O. Box 144, West Sayville, NY 11796.

To access the east side of Shinnecock Inlet from the Montauk Highway, take Hasley Neck Lane 1.3 miles to Meadow Lane. Turn right onto Meadow Lane and go 3.3 miles to Shinnecock County Park East, which is part of the Suffolk County Park System. From New York City, take the Long Island Expressway east to Exit 70. Turn south on Route 111, West Hampton Road. Turn left (east) onto Route 27a, the Sunrise Highway, to Halsey Neck Lane. Then go right (south) on Halsey Neck Lane to Meadow Lane, turn right on Meadow and follow it until it ends at Shinnecock Inlet County Park East.

If you choose not to purchase the Green Key Card, there is easy access to the west jetty through Shinnecock Inlet County Park, which does not have nonresident restrictions. There is a large parking lot and, seasonally, a parking fee is charged. While not as popular with fly-rod regulars, the west jetty does offer shots at false albacore, and it is well worth a try if you don't have a county pass.

To access the west jetty from Montauk, take the Montauk Highway (Route 27a) into the town of Hampton Bays. Turn left onto Ponquogue Road and go 1.5 miles, following signs for the beaches and the Coast Guard station. Turn left onto Shinnecock Road for one-tenth of a mile and then turn right onto Foster Avenue. Go across the Ponquogue Bridge to Dune Road, turn left, and go 1.5 miles to the old Coast Guard station. You can park in the lot on Road H to the right after September 15. Before the 15th, park at Charles F. Altenkirch County Park. From New York City, take the Long Island Expressway to Exit 71 (Route 24). Take Route 24 south to the Sunrise Highway (Route 27). Take Route 27 to the Hampton Bays exit. Then take Route 27a east to Ponquogue Road and follow the directions given above.

Moriches Inlet

Most of the South Shore flyrodders who target false albacore rate Moriches Inlet a close second to Shinnecock. Some years it will even outfish Shinnecock for numbers of false albacore taken. However, it is not as accessible for the walking fisherman. Without an over-sand vehicle and a Suffolk County Permit, the east jetty is a 2-mile walk and the west jetty a 7-mile walk. To reach the east jetty, take Sunrise Highway (Route 27) to Exit 63. Follow Route 31 South, following signs to West Hampton Beach. Route 31 South changes road names several times, but keep following the green signs to West Hampton Beach. Approximately 5 miles from the Sunrise Highway, you will cross a bridge to the barrier island. Turn right onto Dune Road and travel 5 miles to Cupsoque Beach Park in the town of South Hampton. The jetty is 2 miles west on the over-sand road. You need a permit for a beach buggy from the Suffolk County Park System. To access the west jetty, take Route 27, the Sunrise Highway, to Exit 58s. Take Route 46 South, the William Floyd Parkway, for 4.5 miles to the bridge to Fire Island. To the east is Smith Point County Park. Here you will need a Suffolk County pass and an over-sand vehicle to reach the west jetty, which lies some 7 miles to the east.

Fire Island is a 32-mile-long, half-mile-wide barrier island that is managed under the jurisdiction of 17 different towns. Fire Island has three large public fishing areas, each under a different governmental jurisdiction. In addition to Smith Point County Park on the eastern end of Fire Island, the central portion is managed by the National Park Service (NPS) as a national seashore. You can obtain a beach access permit from the NPS to access mile after mile of pristine beaches, which seasonally provide excellent fishing for striped bass and bluefish. For false albacore, your time will be better spent working one of the two inlets.

Fire Island Inlet

Fire Island Inlet, located at the western tip of Fire Island, was once marked by the Fire Island Lighthouse, which was built in 1825 to guide ships into the waters of Great South Bay. As late as 1856, a ship passing through the inlet would come close enough to the lighthouse that they could toss a newspaper to the lighthouse keeper. In the following 100 years, almost 5 miles of sand accumulated between the lighthouse and the inlet. Today, the area from the lighthouse west to the inlet is a New York state park, named after Robert Moses, the visionary designer of the Long Island State Park System and its first commissioner. The best fishing for false albacore occurs at the inlet, which is 1.5 miles from the parking area known as Field 2. False albacore regularly come into this inlet. During the early morning hours or during the week, when there is little boat traffic, albies will come inside the bay as far back as Captree Boat Basin.

To access Fire Island Inlet, take the Long Island Expressway (495) to Exit 53s. Go south onto Sagtikos Parkway, which turns into the Robert Moses Parkway. Continue south over the causeway to Robert Moses State Park. Follow the signs for Field 2. From Field 2, you can walk the back beach looking for breaking fish. It's about 1.5 miles to the inlet. There is over-sand vehicle access to the inlet for New York State Four-Wheel-Drive Permit holders. This same permit covers both Robert Moses and Montauk State Parks.

Jones Inlet

From its very opening, Jones Beach State Park has been the most renowned of all Long Island's state parks. The 2,400-acre beachfront park opened on August 4, 1929, with then-governor of New York Franklin D. Roosevelt heading the list of attending dignitaries. In addition to providing millions of New York City citizens with beach access, the park provided freshwater swimming, diving, tennis courts, a golf course, a boat basin, and a concert stadium hosting world-famous performers. With all these attractions, the park is quite popular, and anglers should avoid it during the peak of the summer season. There is no vehicle access to the beach or inlet, which is about a 1-mile walk from the nearest parking lot. During September and October, false albacore will run the east side of the inlet and along the sandy beach on the back side of the island. Quite often they will run this beach on the last two hours of the incoming tide all the way back to the Meadowbrook Bridge.

To access Jones Inlet from the Southern State Parkway, take the Meadowbrook Parkway south to Jones Beach. After you cross the last bridge, bear right to a large public parking lot known as West End 2 at Jones Beach. The inlet is a 1-mile walk west from this lot.

Breezy Point

Just thirty minutes from Manhattan in the Far Rockaways is Breezy Point, a part of the Gateway National Recreational Area, which is managed by the National Park Service. The jetty at Breezy Point has to rank as one of the best, if not the best, shore locations for flyrodding for false albacore in the Metro area. Shore anglers generally focus on the rip that forms off the tip of the jetty on an outgoing tide, but albies have been known to push bait tight to the jetty on incoming water. Albies also corral bait in the protected pocket against the jetty on the beach side. More than one charter captain reported seeing albies pack the bait so close to the jetty in this pocket that the shore guys out-fished the boat guys by as much as five to one. The jetty is not for the faint of heart. It can be treacherous, and corkers or cleats on your footwear are a must. Because of its close proximity to the city the jetty can get quite crowded, so it's important to get there early. To have a shot at fishing from a prime location on the jetty, you should be in a position to fish at first light.

To access Breezy Point, from the Belt Parkway take Exit 11s, and go south on Flatbush Avenue, crossing over the Marine Parkway Bridge. Bear right following the signs for Breezy Point (heading west). To obtain a NPS Parking Permit, take the first left into Fort Tilden. You can access the Breezy Point Jetty by foot or four-wheel-drive. By foot, park in B222nd Street parking lot; a Fisherman Parking Permit is required. By four-wheel-drive, with the appropriate permit available at Fort Tilden, you can follow the sand road from the parking lot. The jetty is about 1 mile from the parking lot.

Summary of Long Island Beach Access Permits

A New York State Park Night Fishing Permit gives you access to night fishing at Jones Beach, Robert Moses, and Montauk State Parks. Permits are available from January 1 to April 30 and again after Labor Day. They can be purchased at all three parks for $15 at the time of this writing. To use an over-sand vehicle you can obtain a New York State Park 4x4 Vehicle Fishing Permit, which gives you 4x4 access to Robert Moses and Montauk State Parks. Permits are currently available for $39. This also lets you fish at night at the three parks mentioned above.

The Suffolk County Tourist Green Key Card gives you access to parking and 4x4 vehicle access to the beaches of the county parks on both sides of Shinnecock and Moriches Inlets. Write the Suffolk County Department of Parks, P.O. Box 144, West Sayville, NY 11796.

A Breezy Point Parking Permit gives a fisherman day and night access to Floyd Bennett Field, Fort Tilden, and the parking lot at Breezy Point. The Breezy Point 4x4 Vehicle Fishing Permit gives you 4x4 access to the Breezy Point Jetty. Both permits are available at the park office at Fort Tilden at a cost of $25. With the 4x4 vehicle permit, you don't need a parking permit.

New Jersey

The state of New Jersey is, unfortunately, often the brunt of outsider jokes. As a resident of New Jersey and an environmentalist, I admit that New Jersey has some serious environmental issues to deal with, but I am pleased to report that coastal fishing opportunities are not among them. New Jersey has a tremendously diverse coastline, with beautiful beaches, barrier islands, vast bays, tidal marshes, inlets, and famous rock jetties. New Jersey has over a dozen major inlets, and all are easily accessed from the Garden State Parkway. Year in and year out, the northern inlets from Barnegat Inlet north to Sandy Hook provide the most consistent false albacore fishing in the state, so I will limit my discussion of New Jersey's hot spots to the more productive northern locations. In addition to having some very productive inlet and jetty fishing to test your skills, New Jersey also has two large, permanently-protected barrier beaches, Sandy Hook and Island Beach State Park.

Sandy Hook

The tip of Sandy Hook is the northernmost point of the Jersey coast. The nearby Sandy Hook Lighthouse, built in 1764, has the distinction of being one of the oldest lighthouses in America. Sandy Hook is actually a peninsula that acts like a barrier island, buffering Raritan Bay from the Atlantic Ocean. Because Sandy Hook is also the "gateway" to New York Harbor, it has always been a strategic location for national defense. In 1895 Fort Hancock, now part of Gateway National Recreation Area, was established to defend New York Harbor from invading ships. Today, the recreation area has 7 miles of ocean beaches and provides some of the East Coast's best autumn surf fishing.

Generally, the most productive area to fish from shore is the tip of the Hook. To reach this famous spot, known as the Rip, take the main access road north from the entrance to the last parking area (K) at the tip of the Hook. Then follow the Fisherman's Trail, about a fifteen-minute walk to the Rip, which runs right up against the beach. False Hook is another productive spot for false albacore. It's just north of North Beach, and while the shifting sands of the Hook are constantly changing the look of this beach, False Hook always has a good, deep rip tight against the beach. To reach False Hook, park at the North Beach lot and walk northeast toward the water. If the fish are not in the rip line at False Hook, try fishing three-tenths of a mile south at North Beach, which always seems to harbor schools of bait. North Beach has fished well in recent years, and just this past fall, I met a young flyrodder who landed his first nine albies in nine days there. Not a bad average for even a veteran angler.

To reach Sandy Hook, take Exit 117 on the Garden State Parkway. Take Route 36 east for approximately 12 miles into Highlands, cross the bridge over the Shrewsbury River and turn right, following the signs for

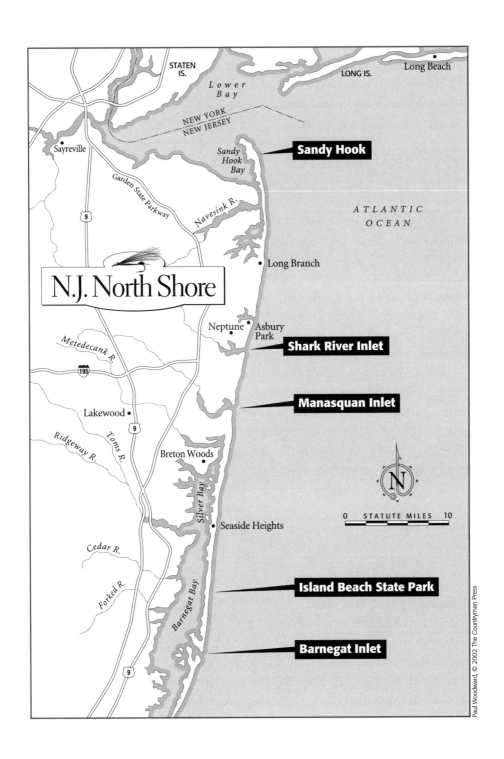

STATEN IS.

LONG IS.

Long Beach

Lower Bay

NEW YORK
NEW JERSEY

Sayreville

Sandy Hook Bay

Sandy Hook

Garden State Parkway

9

Navesink R.

ATLANTIC OCEAN

• Long Branch

N.J. North Shore

Metedecank R.

Neptune • Asbury Park

Shark River Inlet

195

Manasquan Inlet

Lakewood •

9

Ridgeway R.

Toms R.

Breton Woods •

Island Beach State Park

Silver Bay

• Seaside Heights

Cedar R.

Forked R.

Barnegat Bay

Barnegat Inlet

N

0 STATUTE MILES 10

9

Paul Woodward, © 2002 The Countryman Press

Gateway National Recreation Area-Sandy Hook. While there is no four-wheel-drive access, you will need a permit to fish at night or if you plan to fish at first light. An annual fishing permit can be purchased for a $25 fee. You must pay by check or money order, as cash is not accepted.

If you fish between Memorial Day and Labor Day, plan to arrive in the early morning or late afternoon to avoid the traffic jams at the entrance. A parking fee is charged during the summer season.

Jetty Country

In Monmouth County, the area from Sandy Hook south to the Manasquan Inlet is known as "Jetty Country," and for good reason. New Jersey's North Shore has over 120 rock jetties in the first 20 miles below Sandy Hook. An angler could spend a lifetime (and many have) trying to learn which jetty produces fish on which tidal stage and wind direction. Most of the local jetty-jocks target striped bass in the wee hours of the night, and they aren't going to readily give up secrets learned over a lifetime of sleepless nights. However, if the locals realize that you're only interested in catching false albacore, they might disclose where they saw breaking albies at first light when their session ended.

If you're traveling to or from Sandy Hook to the Shark River or Manasquan Inlets, it pays to stop and check for signs of fish from a few of the jetties along the way. A good pair of binoculars just might reveal a pleasant surprise. Every baitfish migrating south along the beach in the fall has to deal with these rock obstacles. The north pocket of each jetty is where the carnage between bait and predator is most likely to take place.

Shark River Inlet

The first inlet heading south from Sandy Hook is the Shark River Inlet. This inlet is about 15 miles south of the Hook. The north jetty is in the town of Avon by the Sea and the south jetty is just across the bridge in the town of Belmar. Both jetties are relatively low to the water and fly-rod friendly. The north jetty is favored by fly fishermen because, in addition to being low to the water, it also has an L shape near the end as it turns north and parallels the beach. This jetty is one of the safer to fish along the beaches of Jetty Country. Shark River Inlet can be boom or bust when it comes to locating albies. It certainly has had its share of good days, but it also gets more than its share of slow days. I generally use it as a backup location when I am fishing the Hook.

To access the inlet from the north, take Main Street (Route 71) in

Lance Erwin with a false albacore landed on the North Jetty at Barnegat Inlet, New Jersey

ED JAWOROWSKI

Avon south to Sylvania Avenue; turn left on Sylvania Avenue for six-tenths of a mile to Ocean Avenue, then turn right on Ocean Avenue for three blocks to the inlet. From the south, take Route 35 into the town of Belmar, and turn right at the third light, which is Tenth Avenue. Stay on Tenth Avenue for six-tenths of a mile to Ocean Avenue. Turn left on Ocean Avenue to the inlet, which is just past the Belmar Fishing Club. Street parking is available on both sides of the inlet.

Manasquan Inlet

Manasquan Inlet is the next inlet south of Shark River, and like Shark River, it too can be boom or bust. Manasquan Inlet is flanked by two jetties that are both high off the water. The inlet has more water exchange than the Shark River Inlet and is very popular with surfcasters. While public access and parking are good on both sides of the inlet, for most anglers, the north jetty gets the nod. You can fish the inlet from the north jetty, and it also gives you better access to fish the ocean side of the jetty. Due to the height of the jetty, it is very difficult to fish with a fly rod, but it is possible. The best fly-rod location is the north pocket, where the beach meets the jetty. Like the north pocket of so many of the Jersey jetties, during the autumn southerly migration of baitfish, predators have an easy ambush location there.

To access the north jetty at Manasquan Inlet, from Route 35 take Union Avenue (Route 71) north to Fisk Avenue. Turn right on Fisk Avenue, which turns into Brielle Road and go 1 mile to First Avenue. Turn right on First Avenue for four-tenths of a mile to Riverside Drive, which parallels the inlet. Park on Riverside Drive and walk to the jetty. Parking and access in Jetty Country can be problematic during the summer season, but both improve dramatically after Labor Day.

Island Beach State Park

Island Beach State Park is a beautiful beach and dune ecosystem that runs 10 miles barrier (jetty) free, starting at Seaside Park and ending at the famous North Jetty of Barnegat Inlet. This barrier island separates the Atlantic Ocean to the east from Barnegat Bay to the west. The parkland was once owned by Henry Phipps, the well-known steel magnate and partner of Andrew Carnegie. Phipps had purchased the property in 1926 with plans to build an upscale, gated, private community. He built the Ocean House, the Bay House, and the Freeman House before the stock market crash of 1929. The market crash and poor health brought an end to his dream of building an exclusive resort. In 1953 the state of New Jersey purchased the park from the Phipps Estate. Today, the park is permanently protected and open year-round for public enjoyment.

Island Beach State Park and neighboring Seaside Park are heavily visited by beachgoers and amusement park lovers in the summer, but in the fall they turn into a surfcaster's heaven. There are plenty of tackle shops, restaurants, and motels that cater to fishermen in the fall. Beach buggies are very popular south of Jetty Country, and on beautiful autumn weekends, Island Beach State Park is home to hundreds of 4x4s. The New Jersey Beach Buggy Association has done a terrific job in working with Park Superintendent Bill Verbitt to give mobile anglers access to this beautiful barrier island without damaging the fragile ecosystem. The association does everything from planting dune grass to installing snow fences in order to fortify the dune system. It also provides 24-hour courtesy patrols during the peak fishing season.

Autumn is prime blitz season in the park. Starting with the first northeastern storm, baitfish come pouring down the beach. During the false albacore run, you can expect to see schools of mullet, silversides, bay anchovy, and young-of-the-year peanut bunker. The false albacore run usually lasts from four to six weeks, beginning as early as mid-August and lasting through October, with prime time being mid-September to mid-October.

Although blitzes can occur anywhere, the gathering place for prey, predators, and anglers is usually at the south end of the park, at the North Jetty of Barnegat Inlet. It's not uncommon to see bass, blues, and false albacore tearing up bait in the pocket where the sand meets the jetty, causing the baitfish to turn out toward deeper water to continue their southerly migration. During these falls blitzes, fly-rod grand slams aren't unusual at the North Jetty.

To reach Island Beach State Park, take the Garden State Parkway to Exit 82, Toms River. Take Route 37 east for approximately 7 miles, crossing the bridge over Barnegat Bay. Exit right and follow the signs for Island Beach State Park. Continue for approximately 3 miles south on North Central Avenue to the park entrance. For fishermen, the park is open 24 hours a day, 365 days a year. There is a daily per-vehicle entrance fee. A paved road runs from the entrance at the guardhouse some 8 miles south to the last parking area. There are numerous parking lots along the road, with paths over the dunes for the walking angler. For beach buggy access you can purchase a 72-hour pass for $25 or an annual pass for $125. To access the North Jetty, drive to the last parking area on the

Landing a false albacore from shore at Island Beach State Park

paved road, Area 23. From here it is 1.5 miles over sand to Barnegat Inlet and the North Jetty.

The Northeast, including the southern end of Cape Cod and nearby islands, the Rhody Breachways, the Connecticut rips, the inlets on the South Shore of Long Island, and New Jersey's North Shore, has numerous inshore false albacore hot spots. South from Barnegat Inlet, inshore fishing for false albacore tends to be sporadic. The ocean speedsters seem to swing wide off the coast and don't normally show up again in good numbers inshore until you reach the Outer Banks of North Carolina.

Fishing Clubs

New York and New Jersey both share a long history and rich tradition of saltwater fly fishing. In the early 1960s, the Saltwater Fly Rodders of America, Chapter One, was founded in Seaside Park, New Jersey. In the 1970s, the club disbanded. In 1987, world-class fly tier, caster, and instructor Bob Popovics started having regular tying sessions in his home in Seaside Park. Every Tuesday night for the next five years Bob hosted tiers from as far away as Pennsylvania and New York. The crowds grew to over 50 people, and in 1992, Bob and several of the regulars formed the Atlantic Saltwater Fly Rodders of Seaside Park. Today, the Atlantic Saltwater Fly Rodders is one of the largest and best-run fly-fishing clubs in the country.

On the other side of the Hudson, another fine club was developing. In 1966, Neil Druger formed The Salty Flyrodders of New York. Today, they are the sole remaining chapter of the original Salty Flyrodders of America. The club is very active and it currently exceeds 200 members.

With all its history and tradition, this region has developed some of the most innovative and creative fly tiers along the Atlantic coast. These include Joe Blados, Glen Mikkleson, Bob Veverka, Bob Lindquist, Enrico Puglisi, Teddy Patlen and Bob Popovics. This incredible pool of innovative tiers has given the region some killer patterns to match the local baitfish.

Naturals and Their Imitations

The most important baits for false albacore in the New York and New Jersey area are bay anchovy, mullet, silversides, and, in recent years, the resurgence of peanut bunker. The most popular pattern in the region, especially when albies are on bay anchovy or silversides, is Bob Popovics's

Surf Candy. The bodies of Surf Candy are tied with synthetics and shaped with epoxy, giving them the translucent look of the naturals. Bob Lindquist's Royal Anchovy is another epoxy variation that is becoming very popular with the guides fishing out at the End. During the September mullet run, Long Island flyrodders arm themselves with Lindquist's Red-Nosed Mullet pattern and Jersey anglers wouldn't be caught without Popovics's Siliclone. To round out your New York and New Jersey fly selections, add Clousers, Deceivers, Popovics's Jiggy, and Joe Blados' Crease Fly.

North Carolina's Outer Banks 13

The National Seashores

North Carolina's fabled barrier islands, known collectively as the "Outer Banks," with their numerous national and state preserves, represent one of North America's great natural treasures. The Outer Banks are most famous for being the location where the Wright brothers made their famous first flight at Kitty Hawk. They are also home to our country's first national seashore, Cape Hatteras National Seashore, which was established in 1953 and covers about 85 percent of Hatteras Island. It encompasses more than 30,000 acres and is over 70 miles long, from Nags Head south to Ocracoke Inlet.

South of Ocracoke and across the inlet is Portsmouth Island, which was founded in 1753. Fueled by the major trade route that ran through Ocracoke Inlet, it grew to be one of the largest settlements on the Outer Banks. Unfortunately, now it is just a ghost town, having been the victim of savage storms, with the final blow being delivered by the hurricane of 1846, which opened Hatteras Inlet. Hatteras Inlet is a deeper, more navigable inlet than Ocracoke Inlet and provided a more northern route to major seaports. It quickly became the route of choice for sailing vessels, which had been the mainstay of Portsmouth's economy. Today, Portsmouth is partially restored as part of Cape Lookout National Seashore, which was established in 1966. It encompasses both Portsmouth Island and the pristine uninhabited barrier islands to the south, known as the Core Banks. With no roads or bridges, no accommodations, and being accessible only by boat, these pristine islands are about as remote a place as you can find on the East Coast.

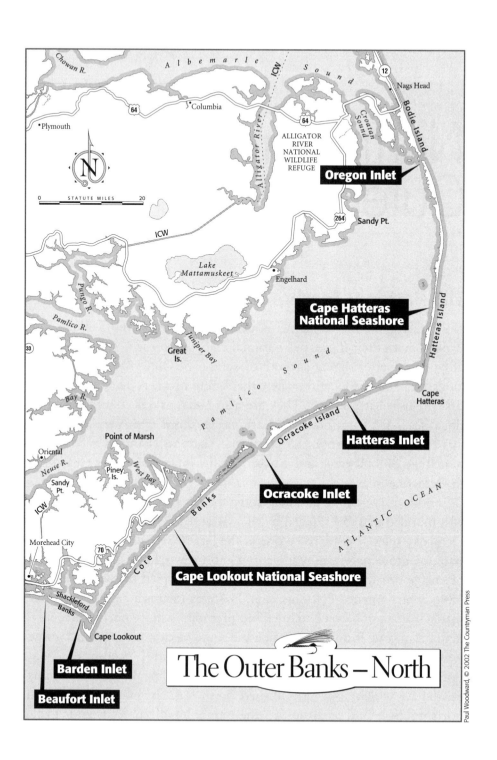

Chowan R.

Albemarle   *Sound*

ICW

12

Nags Head

64

Columbia

64

Plymouth

ALLIGATOR
RIVER
NATIONAL
WILDLIFE
REFUGE

Croatan
Sound

Bodie Island

Oregon Inlet

N

264

Sandy Pt.

STATUTE MILES

0   20

ICW

*Lake
Mattamuskeet*

Engelhard

Pungo R.

33

Pamlico R.

Juniper Bay

Great
Is.

**Cape Hatteras
National Seashore**

Hatteras Island

Cape
Hatteras

Bay R.

Pamlico   Sound

Point of Marsh

Ocracoke Island

Hatteras Inlet

Oriental

Piney
Is.

West Bay

Neuse R.

Sandy
Pt.

Ocracoke Inlet

ICW

Banks

ATLANTIC   OCEAN

Morehead City

70

Core

Cape Lookout National Seashore

Shackleford
Banks

Cape Lookout

Barden Inlet

Beaufort Inlet

The Outer Banks – North

Paul Woodward, © 2002 The Countryman Press

Cape Lookout is at the southern end of the Core Banks. The beautifully-designed diamond pattern of Cape Lookout Lighthouse looks out over Cape Lookout Bight and Barden Inlet, which separates the Core Banks from the Shackleford Banks. In total, the Cape Lookout National Seashore encompasses 56 miles of the southern Outer Banks from Ocracoke Inlet on the northeast to Beaufort Inlet on the southwest. Whalers and commercial fishermen lived on Shackleford Banks until major storms in the late 1890s forced the residents, known as "bankers," to move to safer quarters back on the mainland. Descendants from the horses the bankers left behind still roam freely on the Shackleford Banks.

The international symbol for the Outer Banks is a lighthouse, but not just any lighthouse. The world-renowned Cape Hatteras Lighthouse, often referred to as "America's Lighthouse," has the well-recognized distinctive day mark, the candy stripe or spiral-striped black and white pattern. Originally built in 1799, it was the first lighthouse ever built on American soil to warn ships away from land; all previous lights had been built to mark harbor entrances. The shifting sandbars and shoals off Hatteras Point are known as the Graveyard of the Atlantic, having claimed more than 600 ships. The lighthouse has been rebuilt to make it taller and

ED JAWOROWSKI

False albacore jumping with Cape Lookout Lighthouse in the background moved inland to protect it from the encroaching ocean. Today, it stands at 208 feet, making it the tallest brick lighthouse in America and tall enough to be visible 20 miles out to sea, so that ships can avoid the treacherous Diamond Shoals. Near the northern entrance of Cape Hatteras National Seashore is another distinguishing landmark, the horizontally-banded, 156-foot-tall Bodie Island Lighthouse, built in 1872. It sits just inland of Oregon Inlet and is the unofficial welcome center to the Outer Banks.

If you do journey to Hatteras National Seashore, try to make time to visit the southernmost point, Ocracoke Island. Ocracoke is accessible only by ferry. From Hatteras you take the free-vehicle ferry, which takes about 40 minutes to cross Hatteras Inlet to the northern tip of Ocracoke Island. The island has mile after mile of pristine white sand beaches and no amenities until you hit the southern tip, which is a charming, quaint fishing village. The all-white Ocracoke Lighthouse was built in 1823, making it one of the oldest continually operating lights in the nation.

You can still find vast wilderness, maritime forest and dynamic beach and dune ecosystem complexes on the Outer Banks. Bounded by the mighty Atlantic on the east and one of the world's largest sound and bay complexes to the west, this narrow slice of sand provides access to some of the best shore, inshore, and offshore fishing in the world.

The Fishing

Where the Outer Banks of North Carolina jut out into the Atlantic, the Gulf Stream veers inland, and the area around Cape Hatteras has the warm currents of the Gulf Stream closer to shore than any other location north of Florida. Depending on the direction of the wind and the strength of the Labrador Current, the Gulf Stream can be from 15 to 30 miles offshore. Here, the stream is about 50 miles wide, and a half-mile deep, and its temperature rarely drops below 65 degrees, providing a year-round offshore fishery. The Labrador Current comes down from Nova Scotia on the inside of the Gulf Stream, and the junction of these two ocean-rivers can create some rough seas and some great bluewater fishing. Hatteras is the jumping-off point for some of the best fishing in the world. Large numbers of yellowfin and bluefin tuna winter off Cape Hatteras, providing anglers great opportunities to land one of these ocean monsters on a fly.

For decades, North Carolina has had the reputation of being one of the best surf fisheries anywhere. Northeast surfcasters have long made fall

Matt Born with a North Carolina albie

trips to the unspoiled beaches of the legendary Outer Banks in search of trophy channel bass, giant bluefish, and jumbo striped bass. The surf of the Outer Banks has produced three all-tackle world records, a 31-pound, 12-ounce bluefish, a 94-pound, 2-ounce red drum, and a 13-pound Spanish mackerel.

Every autumn, false albacore come inshore to the beaches and inlets of the Outer Banks, but it wasn't until recently that they got any attention. In prior decades, catch-and-release fishing was rare, particularly in the Carolinas. With their wealth of good-eating fish, it seemed foolhardy to pursue these "trash fish," fish that you wouldn't feed to your cat. That all changed when the fly-fishing fraternity, lead by Tom Earnhardt and several other outdoor writers, started to fish for and write about the vast schools of big albies that congregated off the Outer Bank inlets each fall. The albies come inshore when the water temperature in the shallow sounds drops into the upper 60s and these baitfish nurseries send vast schools of silversides and bay anchovy funneling out of the inlets on their migration south for the winter. At least that's the plan for those that survive the albie gauntlet awaiting them at the mouths of inlets and along the beachfronts.

North Carolina has a large resident population of false albacore that spends most of the year offshore in the waters of the Gulf Stream. They make seasonal runs inshore in the spring and fall to feed. In the late fall, they are joined by northern albies that migrate down the coast.

North Carolina's fish are generally larger than the fish in the waters along the Northeast coast, or "Yankee fish," as Tom Earnhardt calls them. Large albacore sporting double-digit weights are common in the fall, and every year several fish over 20 pounds are landed. Capt. Brian Horsley has a 23½-pound false albacore mounted on his wall, a gift from a well-satisfied client. A 20-pound fish would break all existing fly rod tippet class world records. The all-tackle false albacore record for North Carolina, which was taken off Wrightsville Beach in 1991 by Lyman Kinlaw, Jr., weighed 26 pounds, 8 ounces. During peak season, you can see acres of busting albies at the mouths of North Carolina's inlets and two-man boat catches of 20 to 30 fish a day are not uncommon. Fish can arrive inshore as early as mid-September, but prime time is mid-October to mid-November. Fishing inshore can remain good well into December if the water stays warm enough. Like the false albacore in the Northeast, the Outer Banks fish start leaving at a water temperature of about 56 degrees and are usually gone at 54 degrees.

The geographical position of Oregon, Hatteras, and Ocracoke Inlets affords them little or no protection from the predominant northeast winds in the fall. These inlets can be treacherous for small boats to navigate, let alone fish. Because of its unique geography, Barden Inlet at Cape Lookout Bight offers shelter in most wind conditions, making it a small boat and fly-fishing paradise.

My First Trip

An article written by Tom Earnhardt inspired my first trip to Cape Lookout in November of 1995. I still vividly remember Tom describing a false albacore's blistering run, which causes line to disappear off reels as "tuna melt." While no longer a secret in 1995, little Harkers Island on the Outer Banks was still a sleepy little fishing town. During the week we spent there, we saw dozens of boats and all but a handful were fishing the

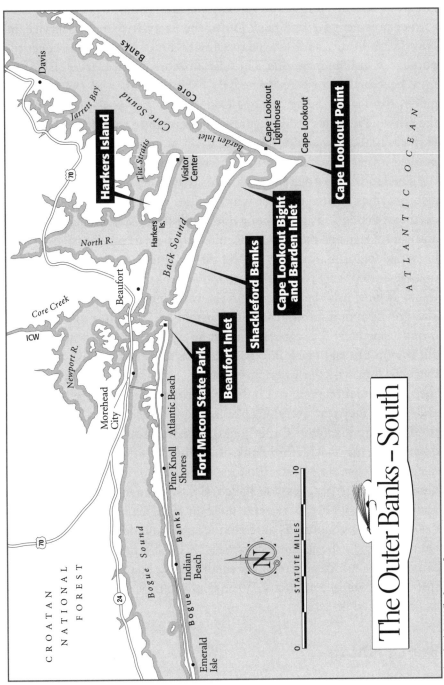

CROATAN NATIONAL FOREST

Davis

Jarrett Bay

Harkers Island

The Straits

Core Sound

Banks

Core

Barden Inlet

Cape Lookout Lighthouse

Cape Lookout

Cape Lookout Point

Visitor Center

Harkers Is.

North R.

Back Sound

Cape Lookout Bight and Barden Inlet

Shackleford Banks

Core Creek

Beaufort

ICW

Newport R.

Morehead City

Atlantic Beach

Fort Macon State Park

Beaufort Inlet

Pine Knoll Shores

ATLANTIC OCEAN

Banks

Bogue Sound

Indian Beach

Bogue

Emerald Isle

N

STATUTE MILES

0   10

The Outer Banks – South

Paul Woodward, © 2002 The Countryman Press

jetty for gray trout. Over the last few years, the fall run has gotten a lot of publicity, with feature articles in popular journals, programs at regional fly-fishing shows, and on national television. In the fall of 1998, former president George Bush joined the party with Secret Service and Navy Seals in tow, and was pictured with a nice albie on the cover of a popular fly-fishing magazine. The false albacore run at Harkers Island has now become a world-renowned fly-fishing event, and every autumn guides from as far away as Cape Cod and the gulf coast of Florida join the growing number of local guides. If you plan to sample the fall run at Harkers Island, my advice is to book early, as guides and rooms are often booked a year in advance, usually by repeat clients.

The Hook at Barden Inlet is a favorite with fly fishermen, as its shape also provides shelter in most wind conditions, especially in north and northeast winds. On an incoming tide, baitfish will seek shelter on the flats and sandbars inside the bight. False albacore tend to run the edges of these bars, picking off bait that is just off the structure. As the tide rises, pods of albies will come up onto these shallow areas to feed. When the feeding frenzy begins, it is sheer mayhem. The water churns white, with busting and greyhounding albies causing constant aerial sprays of frantic bait trying desperately to escape. During these exciting times, if your heart will allow, you can sight-cast into the shallows to individual fish and watch them chase down your offering. Hook into an albie on the flats and their speed and stamina seem to double. There is no down, there is only out, and boy do they tear away! It's like fishing for bonefish on steroids.

The waters around Cape Lookout Bight, from Barden Inlet south down along the Shackleford Banks to Beaufort Inlet, are perhaps the premier East Coast albie destination for both boat and shore fishermen. Behind the barrier beaches you have the vast waters of Core and Bogue Sounds, and all this water and the bait that it produces has to flow through these two inlets. Beaufort is the larger and deeper of the two, providing access for large shipping vessels. Being a large, wide-open inlet, it can often be too treacherous for small fishing boats to navigate during storms and windy conditions. When conditions permit, give it a try, as it can hold a ton of fish.

Boat Fishing

When the weather and fish cooperate, fishing at Cape Lookout consists of looking for birds working over fish busting bait on top. When chased by predators, baitfish increase their schooling density as a defense mech-

DAVE W. SKOK

False albacore busting through bait balls

anism. At Cape Lookout, false albacore often corral several schools of bait into bait balls that can be as large as a basketball court. When the conditions are right, these bait balls are attacked on the surface by false albacore churning acres of water. The Harkers Island area is famous for schools of bait that "stain" the water, with albies chasing them on top. Under these conditions, a fly that perfectly imitates the baitfish might not be effective, since it can't be individually distinguished. Your fly needs to stand out in the crowd. The technique of varying your retrieve to make your offering look wounded or stunned can be effective. A weighted fly like a Clouser or a Jiggy is often belted on the pause between strips as it falls below the bait ball. A popping or skipping surface fly is able to draw attention amid thousands of naturals. My last trip to Cape Lookout provided just such fishing conditions. When schools of bay anchovy balled up on top, well-placed epoxy and silicone patterns drew modest results.

ED JAWOROWSKI

Three anglers hook up to false albacore at Harkers Island

But when we popped Crease Flies into the mayhem, they drew vicious strikes from albies that seemed to come from out of nowhere to track them down. It always pays to experiment.

When wind and weather scatter the bait into smaller pods, the fishing can be more difficult but also more challenging and more rewarding. According to Tom Earnhardt, this is his favorite time to chase what he calls "Fat Alberts." When small wolf packs of 5 to 10 fish are chasing down small pods of bait, you only get a few seconds to deliver your fly. Your casts must be quick and accurate with little or no false casting because you often get only one shot at the melee before the fish disappear. Under these conditions, Tom likes to drop the fly right into the flurry. He points out that in contrast to popular opinion, you really can't predict which way false albacore are going to track. They don't swim in a straight line, and they can turn on a dime and completely change direction. Albies can run in a 360-degree circle or move vertically up and down in the water column. Earnhardt suggests that the best strategy is to get your fly into the area of the bait and keep it there. Albies tend to make repeated raids into the same school of bait, and after each session the school will be a little smaller.

If there is a shortage of prey or if the wind and rough water has scattered the bait, the Harkers Island regulars use chum to bring albies into range. Most of the guides use frozen chum, which can be purchased locally. The chum is usually made up of bay anchovy or silversides, and recent reports indicate that chumming with shrimp heads can also be quite effective. For the best results, you should present your fly with the chum, using a slow, sinking, dead-drift. Chumming can be very effective, but it is not nearly as exciting or challenging as when fish are chasing down a live meal.

If fish are not showing on top, another option is to fish right behind any shrimp trawlers that happen to be around. False albacore forage behind these boats when the trawlers are culling their bycatch. You will usually find bigger fish behind the trawlers, and they will be feeding on bigger bait that gets trapped in the nets. The cull in the waters off the Outer Banks usually consists of a combination of small trout, blues, and croakers in the 4- to 6-inch range. Today, the bigger trawlers are required to have fish exclusion devices, which are supposed to prevent unwanted fish from getting caught in the net. These boats leave a continuous trail of stunned, injured, or dead baitfish in their wake, providing a steady food supply for false albacore. Fishing in these conditions will be down deep in the water column, with bigger flies and sinking lines.

Shore Spots

While most traveling anglers book with guides and fish from boats, Cape Lookout National Seashore provides excellent opportunities for wading fishermen. The National Seashore has no roads or bridges, but there are local ferry services that provide daily shuttles to the outer beaches. False albacore blitz the beachfronts of the National Seashore and the Shackleford Banks within reach of wading anglers, but your best chance of landing them from shore is from the bait-rich inlets.

At Barden Inlet there are several areas worth trying. The flats in front of the Cape Lookout Lighthouse provide great shore fishing when schools of false albacore chase silversides and bay anchovy into the shallows. The area between the rock jetty and the sand spit at the mouth of Lookout Bight is also excellent for shore flyrodders, with the tip of the spit being the most reliable. Beaufort Inlet, the next inlet below Cape Lookout, is wider and less protected than Barden Inlet, but it too can provide excellent shore fishing. On the west side, you can park at Fort Macon State Park and fish the jetty, which can produce on either tide, especially at the tip. You can also take one of the ferries out to Shackleford Point and fish

ED JAWOROWSKI

Two anglers show off their catch at Harkers Island

the sand beach on the east side of the inlet. On the outgoing tide, there is a good rip that sets up along the beach, and this is an excellent spot to intercept false albacore. On incoming tides, the point on the back side of the inlet harbors vast amounts of bait, and false albacore will come in close enough to the beach for wading flyrodders to have opportunities to hook up.

The Pig Roast

Tom Earnhardt started targeting false albacore off Harkers Island in the 1980s. Back then, the killer epoxy and silicone patterns we have today did not exist. At that time, Tom tied up some small Black-Nosed Dace streamers to imitate the resident bay anchovies and silversides, and they worked just fine. For the next decade or so, false albacore became Tom's "secret fun fish." It wasn't until 1994 that Tom came out of the closet. That year, he invited Lefty Kreh, Bob Clouser, and a few other well-known outdoor writers to sample this fishery. One time, after a day of good fishing, Tom invited everyone over to his house to throw a few burgers on the grill. They all enjoyed the fishing and the friendship so much that Tom invited them back the following fall for more Fat Alberts and another barbecue. By 1996, word of the fishery and the barbecue was starting to spread and 40 to 50 fishermen joined in the celebration. Today, the "pig roast" draws over 300 people who, in Tom's words, "would rather fish than watch football on a fall weekend." To Tom's credit, this event, while being a major boost to the local economy, is free from any commercialism. It is attended by a who's who in fly fishing, including writers, tiers, and tackle and boat manufacturers, but it's open to all and, according to Tom, attended by "bankers, bakers, and candlestick makers." Tom's love and appreciation for the region's unspoiled natural beauty and his willingness to literally share his backyard with other albie enthusiasts has gone a long way to promote this great fishery—and how the anglers enjoy it! They have avoided the temptation to have competitions and tournaments, which sometimes bring out tendencies that can put sportsmanship and camaraderie on the back burner.

In the fall of 2001, during an all-out blitz in Beaufort Inlet, I witnessed over 60 boats targeting false albacore with fly rods. The guides came from as far away as Martha's Vineyard and the Gulf of Mexico, and their clients came from around the globe. Almost without exception, all were respecting and cooperating with the other anglers so that everyone could enjoy the spectacle. The anglers were there to enjoy the beauty of the region, the friendship and professionalism of the local guides, and to sample some great seafood. And, yes, to test their skills and tackle with "The Boys of Autumn," who will push both to the limit.

Where Ten-Weights Go To Die

The autumn false albacore fishery in this area is best described in the words of Capt. Sara Gardner, who coined the phrase "where ten-weights go to die." False albacore all along the Atlantic coast are fast, strong, and tough fish, and in North Carolina they can also be big. Sara and her husband, Capt. Brian Horsley, estimate that up to 150 rods have been broken in a single season at Harkers Island. In recent years, repeat clients have improved their landing techniques. For those that haven't, the guides drop down in tippet strength from 20-pound to 12-pound to protect fly rods from breaking. In one year alone Brian and Sara lost 21 fly lines during the fall run at Harkers Island. On the first morning of my most recent fishing trip to North Carolina, I overhead a captain on the radio saying that they had lost all three of the fly lines they had with them. The quick-thinking captain tied leaders directly to the backing and was still able to troll up some albies for his clients.

Several guides reported being sent prototype reels by designers to test before they were put on the market. Many of these test reels never left the drawing boards thanks to the smoking runs of false albacore. Capt. John "Spot" Killen, a Long Island guide who travels to Harkers each fall, reported one unlucky angler who, after hooking into a big albie, had his reel seat break and had to watch as his reel climbed the rod, breaking off each guide on the way. When the reel got to the final piece of his 4-piece rod, it took that section with it as it followed the fish out through the Cape Lookout Bight.

Capt. Paul Dixon reported that he had the pleasure of taking out a couple of clients to test two new prototype reels. A well-known manufacturer had invested approximately $25,000 in the reels. The results? Well, they're not in yet. Unfortunately for the manufacturer, both reels were lost overboard, one on each of the two days of field-testing. The first loss was not exactly a Kodak moment. As the proud angler stood there smiling for the camera with his prize catch, another albie shot by and snatched the fly, which was trailing over the side, taking with it the rod and expensive prototype reel. The next morning, the same angler was chasing another large albie around the boat, and in his haste he tripped on his gear bag. To avoid a mouthful of the boat's fiberglass, he meant to drop his outfit on the deck to brace himself. I'm happy to report that the angler had a soft landing; so did his outfit as it settled to the bottom of Beaufort Inlet, another victim of doing battle with false albacore.

Naturals and Their Imitations

The two most predominant baitfish species targeted by false albacore in the North Carolina waters during the autumn run are bay anchovy and silversides. The bay anchovy run from just over an inch to 3 inches in length. The silversides are generally larger, running about 3 to 5 inches. The local guides feel that any fly is fine as long as it's a Clouser Minnow sized to match the bait.

In addition to traditional Clousers tied with chartreuse, olive, tan, or gray over white bucktail, another very effective variation is the Alba Clouser. This is Tom Earnhardt's pattern, and he ties it with Ultra Hair instead of bucktail. The Ultra Hair gives the fly a translucent body, similar to that of the bay anchovy and silverside. When the albies get picky, Surf Candies can be real killers. Over the last few years, the Crease Fly has also become a local favorite. Not only does it seem to "spontaneously generate" fish, but the visual thrill of an albie crashing a surface fly is unforgettable. For fishing behind trawlers, where the albies will be feeding on bigger baits, the local guides recommend large Deceivers and Half-and-Halves.

Getting There

To fish the waters around Cape Lookout and the Core and Shackleford Banks, you can use Morehead City, Beaufort, or Harkers Island as your jumping-off points. All are easily accessible by taking Route 70 from Interstate 95. Wading anglers can take a local ferry service from Harkers Island to the waters around Barden Inlet or from Beaufort to the Beaufort Inlet and the Shackleford Banks. If you don't have time to take a ferry out and back, you can drive to Fort Macon on Atlantic Beach and fish the jetty. To reach Fort Macon, take the Atlantic Beach Causeway out of Morehead City, to NC Route 58, turn left, and continue past the Coast Guard station until the road ends at the parking lot by the jetty. The nearest public airport to Harkers Island is New Bern, North Carolina, which is about a 40-minute drive from Morehead City.

If you're traveling to Cape Hatteras National Seashore from the southern beaches of the Crystal Coast, take the Cedar Island Ferry, which is about one hour north of Beaufort. This is a toll ferry, which takes about two hours and fifteen minutes to reach Ocracoke Island at the southern end of the National Seashore. Bodie Island is at the northern end of the Outer Banks, and is accessed by Route 168 from the north or Route 64 from the west or Route 264 from the south. Once on Bodie Island, the only road between the islands is Route 12, a two-lane road that connects Bodie to Hatteras Island. The latter is about 45 miles long from Herbert C. Bonner Bridge at the north, which crosses Oregon Inlet, to Hatteras Inlet to the south. It's a beautiful ride down Route 12 with the massive dune system and mighty Atlantic to the east and the beautiful bait-rich waters of Pamlico Sound to the west.

The town of Buxton is near the southern end of Hatteras Island, and the Point, as it's known locally, is a famous surf spot. You will need a four-wheel-drive (no permit needed) to fish here. Or you can continue south by taking the free ferry (a 45-minute ride) to Ocracoke Island, where you can drive another 14 miles to the quaint village of Ocracoke. Once you reach the southern end of Ocracoke, there are no more roads on the Outer Banks.

Florida's East Coast and the Keys

East Coast

These days, the talk of nearly every East Coast fly fisherman, from the Massachusetts Cape Islands to the Outer Banks of North Carolina, is the autumn false albacore blitz. The blitz occurs somewhere along the Northeast and mid-Atlantic coasts from August to November, and each local region has about three to six weeks of solid action (much too short for my liking).

With job and family responsibilities, and the occasional storm, a weekend warrior like myself experiences only a handful of good false albacore fishing days each season. Every winter I used to lament the fact that my next battle with "The Boys of Autumn" was eight months away. Then one day a few winters back, I was reading an article about obstacles in summer offshore trolling (winter is a desperate time for me) and the author, a Floridian, stated: "The day was a disaster; we couldn't catch any decent fish because the boneheads wouldn't leave our lures alone." Boneheads? Could he possibly be referring to "bonito," which is the common name for *Euthynnus allettetatus* in the Sunshine State?

It peaked my interest that false albacore might be found in the southern Atlantic during the summer months, and I started to research the area. I found that the coastal waters off Palm Beach offer a unique fishery. The Gulf Stream passes close to shore there and the absence of a continental shelf means almost everything that swims in the Gulf Stream is close to shore. The area between Miami and Stuart has a virtually continuous reef running the length of the coastline. From Miami north to

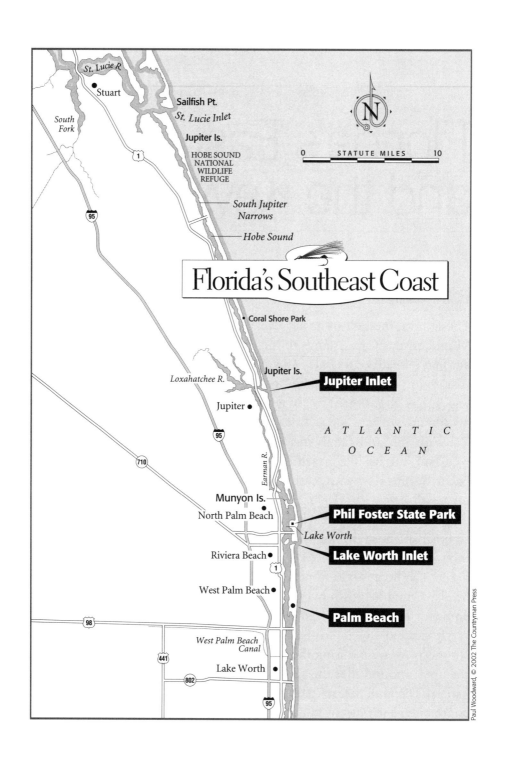

Florida's Southeast Coast

St. Lucie R.

Stuart

South Fork

Sailfish Pt.

St. Lucie Inlet

Jupiter Is.

HOBE SOUND NATIONAL WILDLIFE REFUGE

South Jupiter Narrows

Hobe Sound

Coral Shore Park

Jupiter Is.

Loxahatchee R.

Jupiter Inlet

Jupiter

ATLANTIC OCEAN

Earman R.

Munyon Is.

North Palm Beach

Phil Foster State Park

Lake Worth

Riviera Beach

Lake Worth Inlet

West Palm Beach

Palm Beach

West Palm Beach Canal

Lake Worth

STATUTE MILES

0   10

N

Palm Beach, the reef is about 2 to 3 miles offshore. By the time it reaches Stuart, the reef is 6 or 7 miles offshore. While albies do chase bait along the beach and occasionally come through inlets to feed in the back waters, the focal points for southeast Florida's false albacore are the nearshore reefs and wrecks.

My first few calls to charter captains in South Florida confirmed that the "nuisance" boneheads I read about were, in fact, false albacore. It was evident from our conversations that the guides didn't share my enthusiasm for this fish. They felt that the highest and best use for false albacore was as strip bait for blue marlin and sailfish, because of their virtually inedible dark, oily meat.

My luck changed when I contacted Capt. Scott Hamilton, an offshore fly fishing guide, who works the waters off Palm Beach. Scott told me this area holds false albacore almost year-round. Fishable numbers arrive in late March and stay through August, with May, June, and July being prime time. Unfortunately, my schedule that year did not enable me to book a trip with Scott until the first week in August.

His base of operations is Phil Foster State Park, which is conveniently located on Singer Island, just north of Palm Beach. A typical day fishing with Scott starts with gathering some backup insurance in the form of live chum, just in case the fish aren't blitzing on top. Scott is a master with a cast net, and after a half-dozen throws his 40-gallon live well was loaded with his preferred baitfish, pilchards in the 3- to 4-inch range.

Shortly after we headed out from Lake Worth Inlet, we started passing large schools of busting albacore in the 8- to 10-pound range. Nice-sized fish for this Yankee. However, Scott continued heading north toward the waters off Jupiter Inlet, explaining that he was sure that there was a large concentration of bigger fish, in the 12- to 20-pound range, just north of the inlet. It wasn't long before we could see clouds of birds and the white spray of busting albies. Scott approached the blitzing fish from up-current. After he cut the engine, we could hear and see the violent eruption of albies greyhounding through the masses of pilchards that were being sucked down-tide.

My fishing companion that day, on his first fly-rod outing, was my 18-year-old nephew, Alan Boyd. Alan had done very well the day before practicing his casting on his front lawn. On his first cast, I think a case of albie fever set in, as his fly landed about 25 feet from the stern of the boat. Captain Scott told Alan to let his fly sit while he tossed a handful of pilchards into the water near where Alan's fly had landed. In just a few seconds, the

TOM GILMORE

Capt. Scott Hamilton with Alan Boyd's first fly rod cast and catch

water's surface started to erupt. Alan stripped the line only once and a fish was on. In seconds, the fly line and 100 yards of backing disappeared into the depths below. Alan was hanging on to my 11-weight fly rod for dear life. The expression on his face seemed to vacillate between panic and ecstasy. Eventually, the runs grew shorter as the fish began to tire. Alan was then able to turn the fish back toward the boat and slowly begin to take control of the fight. As the fish neared the boat, the captain was careful to make certain that Alan lifted with the butt of the rod, knowing that "high-sticking," or lifting with the tip, has ruined many a piece of expensive graphite. Scott successfully tailed Alan's first fly-rod fish, a feisty 14-pound false albacore. Not a bad introduction to the world of saltwater fly fishing! After Alan caught his breath and his arms stopped shaking, he confessed that this wasn't going to be as boring a day as he thought. For the next three hours we had nonstop action, with rainbow and blue runners joining in the frenzy created by the live-bait chumming. The following two mornings were carbon copies of the first day. Scott would chum albies into a feeding frenzy and we would catch them until our arms grew weary. Sometimes, a large cuda or bull shark would weigh in for additional excitement. For a change of pace, the afternoons were spent chasing snook, jacks, and dolphin. Due to the closeness of both the reef system and the Gulf Stream, Scott has been able to put his clients onto 33 species of fish on a fly, including king mackerel, cobia, tarpon, blackfin tuna, and even sailfish.

In the last few years, false albacore off the east coast of South Florida have begun to draw the attention of a small following of coastal flyrodders. With the growing number of anglers interested in pursuing the challenge of fly fishing for tuna, many more guides are starting to target them. Today, there are at least a half-dozen seasoned guides that target false albacore in the waters off Palm Beach and Jupiter, Florida.

Florida Keys

Farther south, in the Florida Keys, the popularity of false albacore hasn't taken hold, but that is easy to understand, especially when the blackfin tuna are running. Blackfin are generally available from October to May, with spring being the best time. When the spring blackfin tuna run is in full swing (March through May), it is hard to find a light-tackle captain who will target false albacore. During blackfin time, Keys guide Capt. Jeffrey Cardenas reports that false albacore become "the redheaded stepchildren," and that's the kindest thing I have heard them called in the Keys.

TOM GILMORE

A false albacore caught off the Florida Keys

Both blackfin and false albacore are found along the offshore humps and seamounts. These humps "squeeze" current around and over structure, sending water from deeper layers boiling to the surface along with disoriented baitfish.

One very popular structure for targeting blackfin and false albacore is the Islamorada Hump, a seamount projecting up into the flow of the Gulf Stream about 12 miles off Islamorada. The northbound current of the Gulf Stream pushes against the Hump, forming a rip line. If the fish aren't showing in the current of the rip, charter captains can often bring them to the surface by chumming.

Charters out of Key West fish the Gulf for blackfin and false albacore. They primarily target fish that are around shrimp boats. When the right boat is found, you'll frequently have nonstop action on both species. This is highly visible fishing, with hundreds, and sometimes thousands, of fish on top.

Florida guides that track these fish can be quite resourceful in finding false albacore. Similar to other regions, they look for breaking pods of fish, birds working, or shrimp boats culling their catch. When there is no visible sign of action, guides troll with hookless teasers as you would for billfish, and in these Gulf Stream waters you could very well tease one of these monsters up. When a pod of albies get on the teasers, they reel them into casting range and yank the teaser out and replace it with a fly. Once they have fish around the boat, a steady stream of chum is used to keep them there.

Without a doubt, the best way to start a "session" is with live chum. Almost all of the Florida guides I interviewed told me they start every day by gathering live baitfish. This is usually done with a cast net, but they can also be gathered by using a section of light mono with several gold hooks that the baitfish will hit. It takes a lot of skill, practice, and stamina to accurately throw a net that is 10 or 12 feet in diameter and weighs 15 to 18 pounds. For keeping bait alive, most guides use a 40-gallon live well, with a constant supply of fresh seawater being pumped into the well. On my first few trips to Florida, it was hard for me to be patient during bait gathering, which is often very time-consuming. It usually takes about an hour, but I have seen it take over two hours in poor weather conditions. Bait gathering is hard and tedious, and you and your guide need to work through this part of the trip. Believe me, you won't regret the time "wasted" in gathering live chum after you see the results. The waters off the east coast of Florida are usually very clear, and if done correctly, live-bait chumming will bring you blitz conditions within easy casting distance.

The best method is to keep a small but steady stream of chum in the water. Once the predators key in on your baits, you will be treated to large, violent explosions as the false albacore chase the baits running back toward the boat for shelter. We have had many marathon fishing sessions where we were doubled or tripled up for hours. With this kind of action, be certain that, if you put a rod down, the fly stays in the boat. Just like the unlucky angler I mentioned earlier, I have seen more than one outfit lost or broken when a fish grabbed a fly that was trailing over the side.

Naturals and Their Imitations

The two most abundant inshore baits used for targeting false albacore in the Sunshine State are glass minnows and pilchards. For live-bait chumming, pilchards are the guides' favorite. Pilchards, also called "greenies" or "white bait," are actually scaled sardines and are favored over glass minnows because they are much hardier. Pilchards run around 3 to 5 inches in length, with a medium-wide body, and they are not translucent. The local "glass minnows" are really striped anchovies. They are very similar in appearance to the bay anchovies we see from southern New England to North Carolina. Striped anchovies are very abundant on both coasts of Florida, and like their cousins in the north, this weak-swimming bait is a favorite target for false albacore. They are very difficult to keep alive, but freshly-iced or even frozen, they still make excellent chum. The pilchards are easily imitated with Clousers and Deceivers in all white with just a hint of green or blue on the backs. Surf Candies are excellent imitations for the translucent glass minnows. When the false albacore really get churning on top, nothing is more fun than tossing a surface fly into the frenzy, and nothing works better for me in these situations than a Crease Fly.

For reasons that should be obvious by now, Florida fly tiers, while leaders in designing patterns for tarpon, bonefish, and permit, have not spent a lot of time at the bench creating flies for their "bonito." The one exception is a pattern developed by Capt. Scott Hamilton. Because my grandchildren may one day be forced to read this book, I'll rename Scott's pattern the "Hamilton Special." This pattern uses very durable synthetics and a large 3-D epoxy eye, and it can be tied in a variety of lengths and widths to imitate all of the region's baitfish. It's relatively easy to tie, and a single fly can last through most of a blitz.

Northeast coastal anglers spend much of the year looking forward to fighting false albacore during their brief stay in the fall. I highly recommend that you give Florida's "spring training" a try. I guarantee that you won't be disappointed. The Florida fishery compares favorably to the more northern hot spots, even the world-renowned false albacore fishery at Cape Lookout, North Carolina. IGFA world records (through December 2001) show that the east coast of Florida from Cape Canaveral to Key West holds 11 of the 13 male and female tippet class world records (one is vacant) and six line class records. The only place on the planet currently producing bigger false albacore than South Florida is Saly, Senegal, on the eastern coast of Africa. Here, Odile Robelin set five women's line class records in one week in June 2000. The fish ranged from 23 pounds, 2 ounces to 26 pounds, 7 ounces.

Final Thoughts

Over the last decade, along most of the Atlantic coast, false albacore have risen from the ranks of "trash fish" to become the hottest East Coast game fish for fly fishers. While their status varies greatly from region to region, their fame is definitely on the upswing. In the Northeast, false albacore and their inshore cousin, the Atlantic bonito, have developed a cult following. Prime false albacore waters around Montauk Point, New York and Cape Lookout on the Outer Banks of North Carolina have become world-class fly-fishing destinations. False albacore are also starting to attract attention on the east coast of Florida and in the Keys. They are prevalent throughout the Gulf of Mexico and as more anglers in the Gulf region take up saltwater flyrodding, I predict their popularity there will also grow dramatically.

Unlike so many of our fisheries, the false albacore population seems to be increasing. It is not clear whether this apparent increase is due to their limited commercial value or the decrease in their loss as bycatch from the restricted bluefin tuna fishery. Perhaps global warming of our waters has enabled them to expand their range farther north. The rise could also be due to the increase in inshore forage species as we improve the water quality in our estuaries.

For whatever reasons, their increase in numbers and their growing popularity has been a tremendous boon to the fly-fishing industry. Guides, tackle manufacturers, tackle shops, and local economies are all benefiting from the increasing interest in this fish. A decade ago, you'd have trouble finding a guide to take you fly fishing for false albacore. Today, there are hundreds of guides who will specifically target them. The current challenge is finding one with an opening during false albacore season.

After three years of research for this book, I have found very few definitive answers and have developed many more unanswered questions about the life history of this wonderful fish. Unlike most of the world's tuna, albies currently have very little commercial value, and no major industry is targeting them. Hence, there have been no long-term studies on their migratory patterns. To my knowledge, only a handful of false albacore have been tagged and only one recovered. That fish was tagged in the Gulf of Mexico, off Galveston, Texas and recovered in the Atlantic Ocean several thousand miles away off Ocean City, Maryland.

No research has been conducted on their reproductive biology, growth rate, or life span. Currently, there are no laws regulating their harvest and no major advocacy effort to protect them. The time to lay the groundwork for protecting a sustainable population of a species is when you still have a healthy population. We should be forward thinking and actively start the process of getting this great fish recognized with game-fish status. Let's not wait until someone discovers a commercially-viable use for false albacore to take up this cause. The few sales of false albacore that I was able to document were in the price range of 25 to 50 cents per pound. (These fish were purchased for lobster bait.) False albacore are worth many times more in ecotourism dollars as a recreation fish.

As recreational anglers, we can have a tremendous impact in guaranteeing the future of this species. I urge you to practice sound conservation in your fishing through correct fighting, handling, and release practices. I also want to encourage you to support your local chapter of the Coastal Conservation Association. Several chapters have already called for game-fish status for false albacore and bonito.

Appendix

Guides, Tackle Shops, Fly Tiers, and Sources of Information

Massachusetts

South Cape Cod

The Cape and Islands Smart Guide
www.smartguide.org

Rip Rider Ferry (Monomoy Ferry)
508-945-5450

Fishing the Cape
P.O. Box 1552
306 Main Street
Harwich Commons
East Harwich, MA 02645
508-432-1200

Monomoy Charters
Captain Greg Wiesel
P.O. Box 1262
West Chatham, MA 02669
508-945-2861

Shoreline Guide Service
Captain Bob Paccia
56 Beech Street
Bridgewater, MA 02324
508-697-6253
CaptBobPaccia@aol.com

Martha's Vineyard

The Woods Hole, Martha's
Vineyard, and Nantucket
Steamship Authority
508-477-8600

Martha's Vineyard Derby
www.mvderby.com

Coop's Bait & Tackle
Cooper "Coop" Gilkes
147 West Tisbury Road
Edgartown, MA 02539
508-627-3909

Boylermaker Charters
Captain Jamie Boyle
147 West Tisbury Road
P.O. Box 1986
Edgartown, MA 02539
508-693-7454
www.Boylermaker.com
Boyler@gis.net

Blacklash Charters
Captain Leslie Smith
P.O. Box 879
Edgartown, MA 02539
508-627-5894
backlash@tiac.net

Island Fly Fishing Guides
Beach Guides
Ken & Lori Vanderlaske
RR 1, Box 398
Vineyard Haven, MA 02568
508-696-7551
www.Saltwaterflies.com/islandfly/
mvspringrun@yahoo.com

Island Fly Fishing Guides
Beach Guide
Chip Leonardi
P.O. Box 2036
Vineyard Haven, MA 02568
508-693-6581
chip@flyfishing.com

Larry's Tackle
258 Upper Main Street
Edgartown, MA 02539-0155
508-627-5088
www.larrystackle.com

Nantucket

Nantucket Island Chamber
of Commerce
48 Main Street
Nantucket, MA 02554
508-228-1700

Nantucket Jeep Rentals
508-228-1618

Affordable 4x4 Rentals
508-228-3501

Trustees of Reservations
www.thetrustees.com

Mike Cody
Beach Guide
165 Orange Street
Nantucket, MA 02554
508-325-6043
Cody@nantucket.net

Mike Monte
Beach Guide
P.O. Box 334
Nantucket, MA 02554
508-228-0529

Sankaty Head Charters
Captain Hal Herrick
P.O. Box 681
Nantucket, MA 02554
508-228-3838
www.nantucketfishing.com
hal@nantucketfishing.com

Cross Rip Outfitters
Lynne Heyer
24 Easy Street
P.O. Box 55
Nantucket, MA 02554
508-228-4900
www.crossrip.com

Bill Fisher Tackle
Bill Pew
P.O. Box 975
14 New Lane
Nantucket, MA 02554-0975
508-228-2261
fisherst@nantucket.net

Rusty Fly—Fly Fishing Charters
Captain Peter Sheppard
201 Madaket Road
Nantucket, MA 02554
508-982-5398
capt.pete@rustyfly.com

Rhode Island

The Saltwater Edge Fly Fishing
Company
Peter Jenkins
561 Thames Street
Newport, RI 02840
401-842-0062
www.saltwateredge.com

White Ghost Guide Service
Captain Jim White
Captain Justin White
43 York Drive
Coventry, RI 02816-5975
401-828-9465

Oceans & Ponds
Don & Judy Raffety
Pete Farrell
Ocean & Connecticut Avenue
P.O. Box 224
Block Island, RI 02807
401-466 5131

Connecticut

Connecticut Coastal Access Guide
860-424-3034

Captain Steve Bellefleur
65 Farmholme Road
Stonington, CT 06378
860-535-4856

Lauren "B" Charters
Captain Steve Burnett
1114 Flanders Road
Mystic, CT 06355
860-572-9896

Captain Sandy Noyes
19 Turnpike Park
Norwich, CT 06360
860-886-9212

Connecticut Woods &
Water Guide Service
Captain Dan Wood
6 Larson Street
Waterford, CT 06385
860-442-6343
dwood@ctwoodsandwater.com

Captain Joe Keegan
95 Oak Street
Closter, NJ 07624
201-394-8923

North Coast Charters
Captain Bob Turley
40 San Pedro Avenue
Stratford, CT 06614
203-378-1160
www.northcoastcharters.com

Fairfield Flyshop
917 Post Road
Fairfield, CT 06430
203-255-2896

Rivers End Tackle
141 Boston Post Road
Old Saybrook, CT 06475
860-388-2283
www.riversendtackle.com

New York

Dixon's To the Point Charters
Captain Paul Dixon
19 Pond Lane
East Hampton, NY 11937
631-329-6186
CaptPDixon@Yahoo.com

Natural Anglers
Captain Barry Kanavy
3944 Beacon Road
Seaford, NY 11783
516-785-7171
www.naturalanglers.com

North Flats Guiding
Captain David Blinken
P.O. Box 254
Wainscott, NY 11975
631-324-2860
www.northflats.com

Double Haul Charters
Captain Jim Levison
962 Springs Fireplace Road
East Hampton, NY 11937
631-907-9004
www.allmontaukflyfishing.com
FlyFoto@aol.com

One More Cast Charters
Captain John McMurray
141 Beach 124th Street
Rockaway Park, NY 11694
718-945-2255

Briny Fly Charters
Captain John "Spot" Killen
P.O. Box 170
Westhampton Beach, NY 11978
631-728-2277
Brinyfly@att.net

Dragon Fly Charters
Captain Scott Holder
P.O. Box 12451
Hauppauge, NY 11788
516-840-6522
www.dragonflycharters.com
holders@prodigy.net

Fly-A-Salt Charters
Captain Bob Robl
3 Kilmer Avenue
Dix Hills, NY 11746
631-243-4282
rtrobl@cs.com

Fin Chaser Charters
Captain Dino Torino
38 Berry Avenue
Staten Island, NY 10312
718-356-6436
www.finchaser.com
fly4tuna@cs.com

Shinnecock Guiding
Captain Don Kaye
16B East Tiana Road
Hampton Bays, NY 11946
631-728-8175
Capkaye@aol.com

New Jersey

The Fly Hatch
Captain Dave Chouinard
Captain Dick Denis
468 Broad Street
Shrewsbury, NJ 07702
732-530-6784
www.flyhatch.com
Dave@flyhatch.com

Outback Fishing Charters
Captain Bill Hoblitzell
252 Pond Road
Freehold, NJ 07728
732-780-8624
Biloutback@aol.com

Shore Catch Charters
Captain Gene Quigley
73 Yellowbank Road
Toms River, NJ 08753
732-831-0593
flyfishingcharters@aol.com

Reel Therapy Fly Fishing
Charters
Captain Paul Eidman
9 Williamsburg Drive
Tinton Falls, NJ 07753
732-922-4077
www.Reeltherapy.com
paulfish@aol.com

Ramsey Outdoors
John Roetman
240 Route 17 North
Paramus, NJ 07652
201-261-5000
ramseyoutdoors.com
johnsgonefishing@juno.com

North Carolina

Outer Banks Chamber of
Commerce
P.O. Box 1757
Kill Devil Hills, NC 27948
252-441-8144
http://outerbankschamber.com

Outer Banks Visitors Bureau
Fishing Hot Line
800-446-6262

Chamber of Commerce
801 Arendell Street
Morehead City, NC 28557
252-726-6350

Flat Out Charters
Captain Brian Horsley
Captain Sara Gardner
P.O. Box 387
Nags Head, NC 27959
252-449-0562

Cape Lookout Fly Shop
Fish Finder Charters
Captain Joe Shute
601-H Atlantic Beach Causeway
Atlantic Beach, NC 28512
252-240-1427
www.captjoes.com
info@captjoes.com

Intracoastal Angler
Captain Tyler Stone
190 Eastwood Road, Suite 7
Wilmington, NC 28403
910-256-4545
www.saltwater.com
tstone@saltwaterfly.com

Harkers Island Fishing Center
Motel, Marina and Ferry Service
Last Cast Charters
Captain Rob Pasfield
P.O. Box 400
Harkers Island, NC 28531
252-728-3907
www.harkersisland.com

Calico Jacks
Motel, Marina and Ferry Service
Captain Donny Hatcher
1698 Island Road
Harkers Island, NC 28531
252-728-3575

Cape Lookout Charters
Captain Dave Dietzler
202 Panama Terrace
Morehead City, NC 28577
252-240-2850
www.capelookoutcharters.com
ddietzler@ec.rr.com

Goodwin's Guide Service
Captain Adrian "Buddy"
Goodwin, Jr.
P.O. Box 568
2471 Cedar Island Road
Cedar Island, NC 28520
252-225-7801
afulcher@coastalnet.com

Fly Fish North Carolina
Captain Gordon Churchill
3313 Lorena Lynn Court
Fuquay Varina, NC 27526
919-552-6759
www.Flyfish-NC.com

Fish Trap Charters
Captain Tom Wagner
P.O. Box 88
Wanchese, NC 27981
252-473-2657
outerbanksguideservice.com
fishtrap@beachaccess.com

Captain Dave Rohde
P.O. Box 2023
Kill Devil Hills, NC 27948
252-480-6416
www.fish-riomar.com
riomar1@mindspring.com

Rascal Sportfishing Charters
Captain Norman Miller
P.O. Box 742
Ocracoke, NC 27960
252-928-6111
charterboatrascal@ocracokenc.net

Cape Lookout Ferries
Local Yokel Ferry: 252–728-2759
Sand Dollar Ferry: 252-728-6181
Barrier Island Adventures:
252-728-4129

Hatteras Harbor Marina
Highway 12, Box 537
Hatteras, NC 27943
800-676-4939; 252-986-2166

Oregon Inlet Fishing Center
252-441-6301; 800-272-5199
www.oregon-inlet.com

Ocracoke Fishing Center
& Marina
252-928-6661

Florida's East Coast

Hamilton Fly Fishing Charters
Captain Scott Hamilton
2310 Pinewood Lane
West Palm Beach, FL 33415
561-439-8592
www.flyfishingextremes.com

Blue Hole Fishing Adventures
Captain Scott Hofmeister
Captain Jesse Hofmeister
400 N. Loxahatchee Drive
Jupiter, FL 33458
561-747-2101
capthof@aol.com

Seacret Spot Guide Service
Captain Cliff Budd
6230 West Indiantown Road
Suite #7
Jupiter, FL 33458
561-745-9178
aseacret@seacretspot.com

Captain Greg Bogdan
Sailfish Marina
98 Lake Drive
Palm Beach Shores, FL
33419-8848
561-848-2405

Free Jump Charters
Captain Dave Fawcett
20 Palm Road
Stuart, FL 34996
516-283-7787

Magic Fingers Fishing Charters
Captain Mark Houghtaling
15920 SW 85th Avenue
Miami, FL 33157
305-253-1151
www.magicfin.com

Great White Charters
Captain Edan White
5903 Coconut Road
West Palm Beach, FL 33413
561-689-0491
Floridasportsman.com
fseden@aol.com

Custom Saltwater Fly Tiers

David W. Skok
27 Coral Avenue
Winthrop, MA 02152-1133
617-846-0698
dwskok@msn.com

Bob Lindquist
19 Fairmont Avenue
East Patchoque, NY 11772
631-447-1713

Teddy Patlen
198 Westminster Place
Lodi, NJ 07644
973-772-1312
Tedpat090@yahoo.com

Coastal Conservation Association

Texas
6919 Portwest, Suite 100
Houston, Texas 77024
800-201-FISH
www.ccantl@joincca.org

Connecticut
P.O. Box 290224
Wethersfield, CT 06129-0224
860-529-7878
www.ccact.org

Florida
1890 Semoran Boulevard
Suite 355
Winter Park, FL 32792
407-672-2058
www.cca-florida.org

Georgia
P.O. Box 1699
Reidsville, GA 30453
www.ccaga.org

Maryland
101 Ridgely Avenue, Suite12A
Annapolis, MD 21401
888-758-6580
www.ccamd.org

Massachusetts
4 Middle Street, Suite 215,
Newburyport, MA 01950
978-499-4313
www.cca-ma.com

New York
P.O. Box 1118
West Babylon, NY 11704
887-98-CCANY
www.ccany.org

North Carolina
3701 National Drive
Suite 217
Raleigh, NC 27612
919-781-3474
www.cca-nc.com

South Carolina

P.O. Box 290640
Columbia, SC 29229
803-865-4164
www.charleston.net/org/cca

Virginia

2100 Marina Shores Drive
Suite 108
Virginia Beach, VA 23451
757-481-1226
www.ccavirginia.org

Index

Note: Page numbers in italics indicate photographs.

Books from The Countryman Press and Backcountry Guides

Arizona Trout Streams and Their Hatches, Charles Meck and John Rohmer
Bass Flies, Dick Stewart
Building Classic Salmon Flies, Ron Alcott
The Essence of Flycasting, Mel Krieger
Fishing Alaska's Kenai Peninsula, Dave Atcheson
Fishing Small Streams with a Fly-Rod, Charles Meck
Fishing Vermont's Streams and Lakes, Peter F. Cammann
Flies in the Water, Fish in the Air, Jim Arnosky
Fly Fishing Boston, Terry Tessein
Fly-Fishing with Children: A Guide for Parents, Philip Brunquell, M.D.
Fly-Fishing the South Atlantic Coast, Jimmy Jacobs
Fly Rod Building Made Easy, Art Scheck
Fly-Tying Tips & Reference Guide, Dick Stewart
Fundamentals of Building a Bamboo Fly-Rod, George Maurer
    and Bernard Elser
The Golden Age of Fly-Fishing: The Best of The Sportsman, 1927–1937,
    ed. Ralf Coykendall
Good Fishing in the Adirondacks, ed. Dennis Aprill
Good Fishing in the Catskills, Jim Capossela
Good Fishing in Lake Ontario and its Tributaries, Rich Giessuebel
Great Lakes Steelhead, Bob Linsenman and Steve Nevala
The Hatches Made Simple, Charles R. Meck
Ice Fishing: A Complete Guide . . . Basic to Advanced, Jim Capossela
Imitative Fly Tying, Ian Moutter
Mid-Atlantic Trout Streams and Their Hatches, Charles Meck
Modern Streamers for Trophy Trout, Bob Linsenman and Kelly Galloup
Oklahoma Sportfishing, John Gifford
Small Stream Bass, John Gifford
Tailwater Trout in the South, Jimmy Jacobs
Trout Streams of Michigan, Bob Linsenman and Steve Nevala
Trout Streams and Hatches of Pennsylvania, Charles Meck
Trout Streams of Southern Appalachia, Jimmy Jacobs
Trout Streams of Northern New England, David Klausmeyer
Trout Streams of Southern New England, Tom Fuller
Trout Streams of Virginia, Harry Slone
Trout Streams of Wisconsin and Minnesota, Jim Humphrey and Bill Shogren
Tying Contemporary Saltwater Flies, David Klausmeyer
Tying Flies the Paraloop Way, Ian Moutter
Ultralight Spin-Fishing, Peter F. Cammann
Universal Fly Tying Guide, Dick Stewart

We offer many more books on hiking, bicycling, canoeing and kayaking, travel, nature, and country living. Our books are available at bookstores and outdoor stores everywhere. For more information or a free catalog, please call 1-800-245-4151, or write to us at The Countryman Press, P.O. Box 748, Woodstock, Vermont 05091. You can find us on the Internet at www.countrymanpress.com